Christine would like to dedicate this book to her parents,
Bernard and Suzanne Lariviere—who introduced her to skiing.

And to her sister, Joanne Lariviere Nearing—an inspirational skier
and wonderful sister!

THE Downhill Skiing Handbook

Paul McCallum & Christine Lariviere McCallum

BETTERWAY BOOKS
Cincinnati, Ohio

Other books by Paul McCallum:

The Scuba Diving Handbook
A Practical Self-Defense Guide for Women
Underwater Adventures

Cover design by Rick Britton
Cover photograph by Paul McCallum
Photographs by Paul McCallum
Typography by Park Lane Associates

96 95 94 93 92   5 4 3 2 1

Disclaimer: The publisher and the authors do not assume any responsibility for how the information presented in this book is interpreted or used. The reader is advised that skiing is a high risk activity and extreme caution should be exercised at all times.

Library of Congress Cataloging-in-Publication Data

McCallum, Paul.
    The downhill skiing handbook / Paul McCallum and Christine
Lariviere McCallum.
        p. cm.
    Includes bibliographical references and index.
    ISBN 1-55870-254-7
    1. Skis and skiing--Handbooks, manuals, etc. I. McCallum,
Christine Lariviere. II. Title.
GV854.M2193 1992
796.93'5--dc20   92-16481
                                                          CIP

Acknowledgments

Charlie ... thank you for all the many ski trips over the years!

Val, Shelly, Zuleika, John, Chipper, Gaby, Katrina, Doug, Suzanne, and Neal ... our skiing companions on this project.

Barry Krause, for his generous editing of the original manuscript.

Sno-Zone ... for their excellent hats!

Michel and Pierre Lariviere ... Thank you for everything!

All the instructors of the Vol-Au-Vent ski club in Montreal.

Chantal Henault, Sophie Huot, Johanne Dicaire ... Without you guys, the ski club wouldn't have been as fun!

Contents

1. Why Ski? 9

2. Equipment 13

3. Getting in Shape 27

4. Basic Skills 69

5. The Skiing Environment 93

6. Intermediate Skills 105

7. Advanced Skills 119

8. First Aid 123

9. The Skiing Vacation 135

10. Children and Skiing 147

11. Mental Aspects 159

12. Schools, Clubs, and Instructors 165

13. Competition 169

14. The History of Skiing 173

    Bibliography 179

    Index 181

1

Why Ski?

Here are ten reasons why we think you should become a skier!

1. Adventure: "There's over two feet of fresh powder!" yelled Chipper as the Bell Jet Ranger helicopter blasted through the canyons just outside Valdez, Alaska. He was excited because in a few moments he would be skiing unexplored mountain trails where no one had ever been.

At the same instant, thousands of miles away at Mt. St. Sauveur just outside Montreal, Suzanne Lacroix was about to have the adventure of her lifetime. "Just point your skis downhill and go," yelled Bernard, as Suzanne prepared to take the first ski run of her life on the mountain's bunny hill.

Perhaps more than any other sport, skiing gives you the opportunity to have an adventure from day one. Few things in life are as exhilarating as the first time you put on a pair of skis and fly down your first "run." And the adventure doesn't stop! As your skill increases, you'll always be able to find new challenges to keep your adrenaline pumping!

2. Exercise: If you're having trouble sleeping, try going skiing for a day! Few forms of exercise will improve an individual's strength, flexibility, coordination, and endurance as skiing does. There's no doubt about it: skiing is a physically demanding sport. Fortunately, you'll be having so much fun that you probably won't notice until the end of the day. The fact that skiing is such a fun form of exercise is one aspect that makes it so appealing to many people.

Skiing will improve both your muscle tone and your cardiovascular endurance. To achieve the same results in a gym, you would have to participate in both aerobic and weight training. Skiing has the added advantage of taking place at high altitude, which also helps improve your cardiovascular system.

3. Skiing is social: From the first moment you step into a ski resort, you will be surrounded by other people. In fact, every time you get on a chairlift, you'll be with at least one other person ... perhaps an attractive member of the opposite sex! Skiing is an extremely social sport; and it's set in a fun environment that tends to make people outgoing and fun. Also, most skiers are in fairly good shape simply because they're skiing. If you like meeting new people, few activities are as socially engaging as skiing!

In addition, "aprés ski" activities are also traditionally known to be extremely social. Most resorts feature bars, restaurants, and clubs that offer a host of late afternoon and evening activities that cater to the aprés ski crowd.

4. Travel: Skiing almost always involves some form of travel—either to a local mountain a few miles away ... or to a foreign land.

Regardless of your budget or ability, you'll always be able to find a new place to ski that will involve some type of travel. Imagine skiing at the base of the Matterhorn in Zermatt, Switzerland, or helicopter skiing the virgin powder bowls of Colorado, or skiing forty miles an hour down the icy slopes of Killington, Vermont! Traveling is fun ... but traveling for a purpose such as skiing is even better!

5. Relaxation: Skiing doesn't always have to be a high speed blast down a heart-stopping steep cliff! Some skiers like to sightsee and relax on the mountain as much as anything else ... and few experiences are as calming as spending a few minutes taking in the breathtaking views usually encountered when standing 2,000 feet above the world. In Snowmass, Colorado, for example, the resort has set up picnic tables on the mountain where skiers can relax and take in the pristine environment. Other skiers spend a large portion of their day getting a suntan outside the "upper" lodge located halfway up the mountain. If relaxation is what you're looking for, try spending a calming day on the slopes.

6. It's a family sport: Skiing is one of the few activities in which the entire family can participate. It also has the added advantage of being an appealing sport to children and adults alike. How many other activities can you think of that a sixty-year-old, a thirty-year-old, and a ten-year-old can *all* enjoy equally? If you're looking for an activity or a vacation that your entire family can participate in together, then skiing may be perfect for you!

7. To make money: How would you like to earn your living doing something that's as fun as going skiing every day? All resorts need instructors, ski patrol members, lift operators, and management personnel, in addition to the numerous employees needed by the various hotels, restaurants, and stores located in most resort villages. Few sports can be turned into a career as quickly as skiing. If you like to ski, what could be a better place to work than a ski resort!

8. It's good for your head: Many skiers use the sport as a form of meditation. When you are skiing, it's basically impossible to focus your attention on anything else except skiing! Job pressures, personal problems, and financial worries are all usually forgotten during a day on the slopes. The fact that the sport of skiing takes place in such a beautiful setting doesn't hurt either. Most of us find it impossible to get too stressed out when surrounded by the beauty found on a snow-covered ski slope.

Although skiing is an extremely social sport, you can also do it alone ... even if you are traveling with a group. Unlike some activities (such as scuba diving, which generally requires that you dive with a buddy), skiing can be done in solitude if you wish.

9. To compete: Skiing is an Olympic sport. Naturally, not everyone who gets involved with the sport is destined to become an Olympian ... but skiing does offer a wide range of competitive events for all age groups and skill levels. Slalom, downhill, freestyle, giant slalom, and distance jumping are all popular events. If you're looking for a sport that will enable you to set specific goals through competition ... try skiing!

10. Because it's fun: That's the best reason of all!

2

Equipment

Ski equipment has progressed from the uncomfortable, minimally functional, painful, ugly apparatus of a few dozen years ago to the extremely comfortable, brightly colored, lightweight, functional selection available to today's skiers! The equipment has gotten fun-looking too. Modern clothes, skis, and boots all come in colorful, fashion-conscious designs that are visually exciting as well as functional. In fact, selecting your equipment is part of the fun of becoming a skier. Most large cities have annual "ski shows" and conventions. Attending these shows is an excellent way to see and learn about ski equipment before you buy. The shows are also a good place to find substantial discount packages.

What follows is a breakdown of the basic equipment you will need either to rent or buy when you go skiing.

BOOTS

As with all ski equipment, it's a good idea to rent a few pairs of boots before you buy since there is no better way to find out what features you like, or don't like, in a pair of ski boots than to ski in them! You don't need to be an expert, but what feels good in the store might not feel good after a few runs. Actually, this is especially true if you're going skiing for the first time, since you don't have the experience to judge what style of boot is the most comfortable for you.

When buying ski boots, the three things you should keep in mind are: fit, fit, and fit. When you try a boot on, it shouldn't hurt your foot at all. If it jabs or pinches your foot in the store, imagine what it will feel like on the slopes! Also, don't let the salesman convince you that he can "adjust" the boot by adding wedges or by shaving down the inside of the boot's shell.

Ski boots are made up of two parts: *the outer shell* and *the inner lining*. The outer shell really governs how the boot will feel and function. The inner lining basically fills up the excess room inside the boot and is replaceable. One fact to keep in mind is that some manufacturers use one size shell for two or three different shoe sizes and fill up the extra space with the inner lining. Obviously, if you wear a size 9 ½, you want to avoid a size 11 shell with a 9½ inner lining. If you encounter a large-looking boot that feels "spongy" inside, ask the salesman if that particular manufacturer uses the same size shells for more than one shoe size. If so, get the shell that's closest to your foot size.

A custom-made inner lining can be designed specifically for your foot. Skiers who have gone this route claim the custom inner lining makes a huge difference in the areas of comfort and fit.

Ski Boot Features

Some of the features to consider when buying a pair of boots are:

Number and type of buckles. Most boots use between one and five buckles. The number of buckles has an effect on how many ways the boot can be adjusted around your foot.

Another consideration: Can you manipulate the boot's buckles easily while wearing them? You need to be able to operate them when your hands are cold. Keep in mind that when you're wearing skis, your movement is somewhat restricted. For example, adjusting a buckle or knob at the back of your boot may be easy in the ski shop, but will it be easy at the top of the mountain with skis on?

Type of entry. There are currently two basic types of boots on the market: *rear entry* and *front entry*. Which type you go with is really dependent on what type fits you better. Generally, if you like the idea of a "one buckle boot," a rear entry boot may be your best choice. On the other hand, if you want more buckles, then a front entry may be for you.

Rear entry boots usually have some alternate ways of adjusting the amount of tension on your foot. Often, these are in the form of knobs with pop-out handles so you can easily turn them. Some skiers prefer this type of arrangement over the multiple buckle design.

Forward pitch. The amount of forward pitch a boot has determines how you will stand in your skis. It can also determine how much pain you will, or will not, experience. Generally, novice skiers should avoid boots with *excessive* forward pitch. Why? Because in a boot with lots of forward pitch you can't stand upright ... at all. The result is calves that feel like they're on fire! On the other hand, for a racer or an advanced skier, a large amount of forward pitch is a desirable and sought-after feature since it helps maintain a forward bend in the legs.

Flex. Can you bend forward? Do the front of the boots feel like they are digging into your shins, or do they "flex" a bit? When you ski, you will be bending your knees and leaning forward; your boots should allow you to do this without causing pain to your shins.

Height. How high do the boots come up your leg? *One of the main functions of a ski boot is to provide support for your ankles.* Low-cut boots don't provide enough support and generally should be avoided.

Mechanical Adjustments

In addition to buckles, some ski boots also have a variety of mechanical devices that allow you to "fine-tune" various aspects of the boot's fit. Some of the more common are:

1. *Forward Lean Adjuster:* This allows you to set manually the amount of forward pitch (see forward pitch above).

2. *Cant Adjustment:* A cant is a wedge that used to be inserted (and sometimes still is) into a person's boot if their legs weren't perfectly straight (such as someone who is bowlegged). Cants aren't used much today since many boots offer a mechanical cant adjustment.

   Another way of dealing with canting is to use a *cantable sole*, which compensates for the foot's misalignment.

3. *Adjustable Arch:* This device allows you to lower or raise the arch support in the boot.

4. *Heel Elevator:* This device raises or lowers the shell under your heel. The Heel Elevator and the Forward Lean Adjuster can both be used together to adjust the amount of forward lean.

Expect to pay between $200 and $550 for a good pair of ski boots. For example, Nordica's novice boots average $195 ... their recreational, sport, and intermediate boots cost between $250 and $300 ... while their high performance models come in around $400. These prices are fairly typical of most manufacturers.

Here's one last thought to keep in mind when shopping

for boots. Many professional skiers ski in boots at least one size smaller than their street shoe size, the reason being that most pros feel it gives a better, more snug, more adjustable fit since ski boot sizes tend to run a little large.

BOOT BAG

To protect your boots when you travel, you may want to buy a boot bag. Boot bags range in price from $20 to $100 and are a good investment considering what ski boots cost!

Large boot bags have the advantage of allowing you to pack other items (such as gloves, hats, and ski pants) in them. Many skiers prefer this type of bag because it provides additional "padding" around the boots during transit.

SKIS

Don't buy a pair of skis until you've taken a few lessons. Why? Because chances are you will start out on short skis and rapidly progress to longer ones. If you buy skis before taking a few lessons, you will either end up with skis that are too long, making learning difficult, or you'll be talked into buying short skis to learn on, which you will outgrow (ability-wise) after a few hours of instruction.

Before you buy skis, keep this thought in mind: You can't tell anything about how a ski performs unless you ski on it! Ski shops know this and usually have in their rental department the brands they sell for this very reason. Granted, a salesman's opinion can be valuable. But, he does not ski like you do ... and he may also conveniently "love" the brand of skis the shop happens to carry.

Types of Skis

Skis are described with names that indicate the style of skiing and type of skier the ski was designed for. Knowing these categories is important since it will aid you in selecting a ski that's best for your specific skill level, your style of skiing, and the conditions you usually encounter. Some of the more common styles are:

Novice or Learner. These skis are designed with the novice in mind and are a bit wider than most skis. The extra width helps students maintain their balance during the first few hours of instruction. Generally, you want to rent this type of ski rather than buy it since you will most likely outgrow it rapidly. Prices range from under $200 to about $330.

Blizzard's VX9, priced at $195, is one of the more popular in this category.

Recreational. As their name implies, these skis are designed for easygoing all-around skiing. Generally, they're aimed at the novice skier who has mastered the basics, and thus they offer a soft, forgiving ride. Skis in this category often don't hold an edge well on hard pack and may be unstable at high speeds—which generally isn't important to a beginning skier. If you've just learned to ski and are looking to buy your first pair, this type of ski may be a good choice. Prices range from $225 to almost $400. Atomic's ACS 70, priced at $250, and their ACS 80, priced at $300, are typical.

Sport. Skis described as "Sport" are also a good choice for a first purchase. In fact, the terms "Sport" and "Recreational" are often used interchangeably. Generally, a sport ski is a good all-around ski aimed at the experienced beginner. Prices are comparable to recreational skis.

Slalom. Slalom skis are designed for quick turns on packed snow. Intermediate through advanced skiers will find suitable skis in this category. If you like to ski fast and fairly aggressively on hard pack or ice, with lots of turns, then this type of ski may be for you.

Slalom skis that are designed for an intermediate/ advanced recreational skier (versus a racer) will usually be referred to as a *Recreational Slalom* ski. Recreational Slalom skis are softer and easier to turn than regular slalom skis. Recreational slalom skis are currently the most popular style ski on the market since they offer fairly high performance on a variety of conditions. Prices range from $450 to over $600. Atomic's ARC 833 SL, priced at about $450, is a favorite of many slalom skiers.

Giant Slalom. These skis are a bit softer than regular slalom skis and thus offer a gentler ride ... the liability being they're not as "snappy" in fast turns. Giant slalom skis are an excellent high speed recreational ski for someone who skis a variety of conditions. Giant slalom skis are also a good choice for high speed "cruisers." Giant slalom skis that are designed for the intermediate skier are usually referred to as *Recreational Giant Slalom*. Prices range from $450 to $700. Atomic's ARC 835 RS-G, priced at $500, is an excellent high speed cruiser.

Mogul. Mogul skis, designed to be used in the bumps, usually have soft tips that can "absorb" the bumps. Otherwise, mogul skis are similar to slalom skis and offer high performance. Prices range from $350 to around $500.

Downhill. Downhill skis are designed for stability at high speeds. Generally, they're hard to initiate a turn with, and they come in lengths of at least 210cm. Downhill skis are for experts who have the technique to handle the high speeds these skis perform best at without hurting themselves or others. Prices range from $550 to $700. Atomic's ARC 500 AF K and ARC 400 AF K, priced at $550, are typical.

All Terrain. This is a term often used to describe an advanced/intermediate ski that, as its name implies, will perform well on a wide variety of conditions. Skis in this category don't offer as much performance as a Slalom ski, but will be easy to turn and generally fairly forgiving. All Terrain skis are a good choice for a strong intermediate skier who goes on a ski vacation every year, but doesn't know what type of conditions he will encounter. Prices range from $350 to over $600.

Powder. As the name implies, skis in this category perform best in powder. These skis are soft and a bit wider than most skis. Prices range from $500 to over $700. Atomic's Powder Plus ski, priced at $499, is an excellent choice.

Light Expert. This is a fairly new category that refers to skis made for advanced skiers who weigh less than 130 pounds. They're also ideal for expert children. Skis in this category are soft, which means they require less effort to turn. Prices range from under $300 to over $600.

Ski Features

When shopping for skis, it's helpful to have an understanding of how the various aspects of a ski's design affect its performance. Some of the more important are:

Length: Long skis are more stable than short skis since they aren't deflected by bumps in the terrain as easily as a short ski is. Short skis, on the other hand, are easier to turn, can make tighter turns, and are easier to learn on.

Camber: Skis have a bowed shape, or "camber," built into them. How much camber a ski has can be seen by laying the ski down on a flat surface, or by holding a pair together with the bottoms facing each other.

What the camber does is distribute the weight of the skier along the entire length of the ski rather than just under the skier's foot. How much camber your skis have, along with how much compression is needed to flatten them, depends largely on your weight and the type of skiing you do. For example, a 230-pound man would require skis with a stiff camber to accommodate his weight ... while a 100-pound woman would use skis with a much more easily compressed camber.

Flex: Flex describes how resistant a ski is to bending along its length. Usually ski designers vary the amount of flex a ski has along its length at different points.

Generally, stiff skis are preferred by high speed and advanced skiers since a stiff ski is more stable than a soft one. Soft skis, on the other hand, are easier to turn and more maneuverable.

Side Camber or Sidecut: The amount of side camber a ski has affects how it will perform when turning. Generally, downhill skis have very little side camber, while slalom and recreation skis have more. A ski's "dimensions" refer to its side camber and are usually stated in millimeters measured across the front, middle, and back of the ski.

Side camber improves a ski's performance in a turn by helping distribute a skier's weight along the entire edge of the ski, rather than just under the skier's foot.

The disadvantage to side camber is that it takes away from a ski's tracking ability when going straight at high speed. Excessive side camber tends to make skis "drift" uphill in a traverse.

Torsional Stiffness: Torsion describes how stiff or soft a ski is. A ski with a torsion of .88 is relatively soft, while a ski with a torsion of 2.27 is said to be stiff. The measurement is used to describe how resistant a ski is to twisting.

When the front of a ski hits a bump, it has to have the ability to "twist" with the terrain without throwing the skier's foot out of alignment. A ski with a soft torsional stiffness will have a smoother ride than a stiff ski because a soft ski will "absorb" minor bumps in the terrain. A stiff ski, on the other hand, will ride harder since it will be deflected by minor bumps in the snow.

Damping Ability: A ski's damping ability is its ability to absorb vibration. Damping becomes important when skiing on ice or hard pack since it helps the bottom of the ski stay in contact with the snow. A ski with poor damping will be continuously losing contact with the ground—resulting in poor control.

Damping isn't as important, however, when skiing in powder or soft snow because the ski won't be hitting hard obstacles that cause vibration.

BINDINGS

A ski *binding* must attach your foot securely to your ski; it must also release your foot from the ski during a fall. Designing a mechanical device that will hold a skier to his skis and not release under the extreme pressures created when a skier turns, jumps, and hits bumps, but will release during a fall if an injury is imminent, must have been a designer's nightmare! Fortunately for us, modern ski bindings perform these two tasks almost flawlessly.

One of the most important questions you should ask when considering a binding is what *weight range* the binding is designed for. Most manufacturers make a wide range of models and some less expensive ones may not be capable of handling heavyweight people. Marker's M28 (about $100), for example, is not rated for a 250-pound skier—while Marker's M48 ($215) is.

Some other considerations and terms you may hear when shopping for bindings are:

Din Scale: All bindings have an adjustable din scale, which allows the ski shop to adjust mechanically how much stress the binding will endure before it releases the skier's foot. Setting the din scale to one, for example, will release the skier's foot as soon as the skier encounters trouble. Setting the din scale to ten, on the other hand, would result in the binding not releasing until fairly strong forces are present. A skier's weight also has bearing on where the din scale will be set.

Don't try to set the din scale by yourself. Ski shops have ways of calculating what setting is best for your weight and ability, and the type of skiing you do.

Forward Pressure: The heel piece of most bindings pushes the skier's boot forward to hold the toe in the binding's toe cup. The heel also has the ability to move slightly forward and aft to adjust as the ski flexes when in use.

Elasticity: A binding's elasticity describes how far a boot has to travel before the binding releases. If pressure on the boot (such as the ski twisting during an easy fall) is released before the boot reaches the end of its elastic travel, the boot will return to its normal position and the binding won't release. If, on the other hand, the boot travels to the end of its elastic travel, it will release from the binding.

Full Spectrum Twincam: The term comes from Marker bindings but is a feature offered by many manufacturers. A toe cup that is described as "Full Spectrum" generally means the toe can be released by upward pressure in addition to the more conventional side twisting release.

Power Compensation Toe: Tyrolia coined this term to describe the toe piece of their models, which automatically adjusts for the height of a boot's toe.

Operation: How easy is the binding to operate? Some models require bending over to pull or open some type of lever before you can step out of them. Others, such as Marker bindings, are released by pushing down on the back of the binding, which can easily be done with a ski pole. Check out how the binding operates before you buy it.

Binding Maintenance

Considering how important it is to have bindings that work flawlessly to avoid injury, you should have them serviced once a year—ideally, at the beginning of the ski season. Also keep in mind that as your skiing ability increases and/or as you gain or lose weight, you'll need to have the binding's din scale adjusted.

Some ski shops won't adjust, mount, or service bindings that are "old." Some define ten years as old, although each shop may define "old" differently. The reason is that their insurance won't cover them if an injury should result from the binding failing to operate correctly. Considering this fact, you may want to avoid purchasing used bindings unless you can have them checked out by a qualified technician to determine their age and remaining operational life span.

Some of the larger manufacturers of bindings are Ess/Atomic, Marker, Tyrolia, Salomon, Geze, and Look. Bindings made by these manufacturers are all excellent. Expect to pay between $100 and $250.

SKI BAG

Unless you live at the base of a snow-covered mountain, going skiing will always involve some form of travel. Airport baggage handlers, baggage conveyer belts, backs of cars, tops of cars, and hotel porters all love to chip and nick new skis. Investing in a ski bag ($50 to $100) will go a long way towards providing your equipment with the protection it deserves.

One feature you may want to look for when selecting a ski bag is a shoulder strap. If you have to carry your skis any meaningful distance, you'll appreciate the convenience a shoulder strap provides.

You should invest in a ski bag to protect your skis when traveling.

POLES

Okay, *poles* are easy. You can buy them right away and you don't need to rent them first. The important consideration when buying poles is to obtain them in the right length. If your forearm is parallel to the floor, it's the right length.

You may encounter poles that are curved instead of straight. These types of poles are aerodynamically designed for racers who want to cut down on wind resistance as much as possible. Generally, recreational skiers don't benefit from this type of pole design.

There are also poles that are bent along some portion of their length to adjust to where the pole will "plant" in relation to the skier's body. The Kerma Equipe pole, priced at $80, is one example, and also features a Velcro™ breakaway strap.

Most poles cost somewhere between $30 and $80.

GLOVES

A good quality pair of *gloves* or *mittens* is essential to avoid frostbite when skiing. Generally, mittens are warmer than "fingered" gloves, so if you're going to be skiing in an extremely cold climate you may want to go with mittens.

One solution for maximum warmth is the "Hot Glove," made by the Heat Factory at 2334-F Madero Road, Mission

Viejo, CA 92691. Their phone number is (714) 472-8928. The Hot Glove has a zippered compartment in which you can insert a small heat pad if additional warmth is needed. The gloves can also be used without the heat pads if so desired.

Expect to pay between $25 and $100 for a pair of ski gloves.

HATS

Ski *hats* come in a dazzling array of designs and colors. One of the best is made by *Sno-Zone* at 161 Plaza La Vista, Camarillo, CA 93010. Their phone number is (805) 388-1001.

What makes Sno-Zone hats better than most is the fact that they can be adjusted to be worn in many configurations. On a cold day, the hat becomes a full face mask; if the weather heats up, a quick fold and the hat become a "normal" ski hat. Sno-Zone hats can also be turned into neck wraps and head bands.

Expect to pay between $10 and $100 for a ski hat.

GLASSES AND GOGGLES

It's essential that you wear a pair of *glasses* or *goggles* when skiing. Your eyes need protection from the sun, the blindingly bright snow, the cold air hitting your eyes as you ski, particles of snow and ice in the air, snow blowers, and snow on the ground when you fall!

Whether you wear goggles or glasses will depend primarily on the day's conditions. Generally, glasses are all that is needed when it's fairly warm out. Goggles become essential when it is snowing or cold enough that you need to protect your eyes from the wind chill created by your forward motion.

When buying glasses or goggles, ask the salesman what color lens is best for the condition you expect to encounter. Most brands come in a variety of lens colors, each designed for a specific type of snow and weather conditions.

If you are only going to buy one pair, I recommend you get goggles over glasses since the glasses won't offer adequate protection when it's snowing. Glasses and goggles can get expensive. If you plan on getting eyewear that offers UV protection (and you should), expect to pay between $50 and 250!

One new addition to the eye wear market is the "night

vision" glasses made by Uvex (about $42), which are specifically designed for use under the artificial light of ski areas that offer night skiing.

If you wear prescription glasses, you can have your prescription put into both your ski glasses and goggles. The cost will be about $100.

SKI SUITS

To avoid getting wet and cold while skiing, you should buy a *ski suit*. Ski clothing is vastly superior to "normal" outdoor clothing and offers unequaled environmental protection in addition to being made of an extremely lightweight material.

Jump Suits

For maximum warmth, protection, and dryness, consider getting a one-piece jump suit such as the ones made by Descente, Killy, or Obermeyer. Prices range from $200 to close to $1,000. One reason a one-piece suit is preferred by many skiers is the fact that there's no "open waist" for snow to get into when you fall.

Some questions you should ask the salesman when buying a ski suit are:

Is the suit waterproof? Naturally, it should be.

Does the suit "breathe"? Some suits are made of a "breathable" material that helps prevent overheating in addition to allowing sweat to evaporate. Some of the cheaper brands don't use a breathable material.

Is the material resistant to tearing? Look at the suit's label —some will state if the material is tear-resistant. Considering the fact that skiers do occasionally fall and slide a hundred feet (or more), the merits of a suit that won't shred off your body are obvious!

Snow Pants

An option to wearing a one-piece suit is to buy a pair of *snow pants*, which are basically waterproof pants. As with a jump suit, you wear the pants over long underwear. Snow pants come in a variety of styles.

Stretch pants are thin, tight snow pants that offer optimum wind resistance. Many skiers feel that stretch pants are the most comfortable because they're the least bulky of all the snow pants. Stretch pants, however, aren't as warm as the bulkier snow pants.

Powder pants is the name usually given the bulky snow pants. Next to a one-piece ski suit, powder pants offer the most warmth. Powder pants are a better choice for novice skiers than stretch pants since novice skiers may spend a lot of time falling and sitting in the snow. Since stretch pants are thin, they offer almost no protection from the cold when sitting in the snow.

SKI JACKETS AND PARKAS

Regardless of whether you wear a one-piece suit or dress in layers, you'll need a *ski jacket*. Generally, the difference between a jacket and a parka is that a parka is longer and also covers part of the skier's lower body. All the considerations about waterproofing, breathability, and tear resistance mentioned above also apply when buying a jacket or a parka.

Another feature you may want to consider when buying a jacket or parka is a *hood*—you may or may not want one. Also, can the pockets be closed by means of a zipper or snaps? Having the contents of your pockets empty out every time you take a fall can be annoying, as can having snowballs form in your open pockets after a fall.

When trying any type of ski clothing, make sure it will fit when you're in "skiing position." Bend over, sit down, twist backwards, swing your arms around. Make sure the clothing doesn't restrict your movement in any way.

LONG UNDERWEAR

If you live in an area that has an extremely cold winter, you're most likely already familiar with the merits of *long underwear*! For Florida and southern California residents, however, the concept may be foreign.

When buying long underwear, check out the feel of the material. With the amount of movement involved in skiing, you don't want to wear anything that may cause chafing or irritation. Also avoid any underwear that is bulky or has large seams around the neck, wrists, or ankles. Your ski suit will insulate you against snow in these areas, not your underwear.

Long underwear can be bought either as a one-piece suit or the more conventional two-piece outfit made up of a separate top and bottom. The advantage of the one-piece underwear is that it is warmer ... and you don't worry about the bottoms sliding down during your ski day. On the other hand, wearing two-piece underwear makes going to the bathroom a bit easier. Expect to pay between $25 and $100 for long underwear.

SKI SOCKS

If your feet are cold, you won't enjoy skiing. Wearing one pair of large bulky socks may cut off your circulation, which will result in cold feet. Thin socks, on the other hand, don't offer enough insulation against the cold. For most skiers the solution is to wear two pairs of socks—an extremely thin pair followed by a heavier "ski sock." The thin sock allows your foot to move freely inside the thicker sock in addition to providing warmth by "layering" your foot. The thicker outer sock provides insulation against the cold. Expect to pay between $12 and $40 for a good pair of ski socks.

3

Getting in Shape

Skiing is a very physical sport and it is a terrific way of getting in shape—even if you don't do any other exercise! However, most of us don't have the luxury of skiing more than a few weeks each season. Rather than use up those precious few weeks getting back into shape, why not do a few exercises *before* you go skiing so that you can get the most out of your time on the slopes. After your first day on the slopes following a long off-season, you don't want to be so stiff that you can hardly ski the next two days! Get yourself in shape for the coming season by doing a few leg lifts and sit-ups. It can go a long way towards getting you ready.

You don't need to do all the exercises pictured—just pick a few and start with those. Also, if you haven't done any exercise in a while, start off easy. If you think far enough in advance, you can begin to exercise a few months before your first ski trip and build up those thigh muscles and strengthen the knees gradually. And remember, *if you feel anything pulling or hurting, stop!*

Be sure to give yourself a long warmup. Some of the simpler exercises shown, such as the neck, shoulder, wrist, and ankle rolls, are all ideal for this purpose. Also, don't forget to cool down after you have completed the more strenuous exercises. Doing long, slow stretches is a good way to cool down tight muscles.

Most important, be sure to consult a physician before beginning any exercise program.

HEAD ROLL

1. Stand upright and facing forward.

2. Gently roll your head to the left …

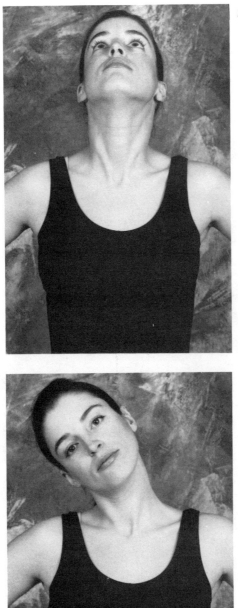

3. ... and to the back ...

4. ... and to the right ...

5. … and to the front.

ARM ROLL

6. Stand in an upright position with your arms held out to your sides.

7. Roll your arms in a forward circle.

8. After you do a few circles, reverse directions.

9. Be sure to make full circles without jarring your joints.

ARM PRESS

10. Stand in an upright position with your arms held as shown.

11. Start to press your elbows together. Pretend you're pushing against resistance.

12. If you can, bring your elbows and forearms together.

13. Slowly return to an open position—again working against an imaginary force.

SHOULDER RAISE

14. Stand upright with your arms at your sides.

15. Raise your shoulders.

SHOULDER ROLL

16. From the start position shown ...

17. ... roll your right shoulder upward ...

18. ... then to the back ...

19. ... and back to the start position. Now repeat the exercise in the other direction.

ARM STRETCH

20. With your left arm, hold your right as shown.

21. Now *gently* straighten your arm and pull it towards your chest.

22. Repeat the exercise with the other arm.

23. Don't overdo the stretch. If you feel pain, stop.

ANKLE ROLL

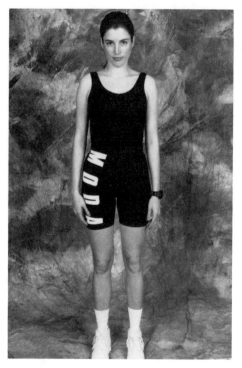

24. Stand in a comfortable upright position.

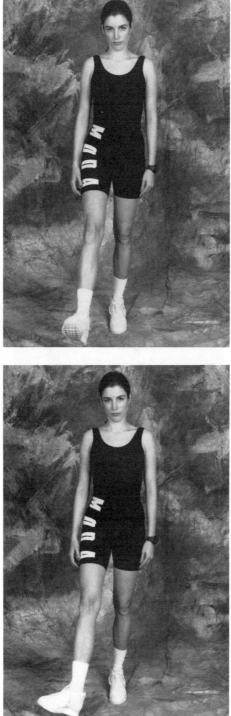

25. Lift your right leg and pull your toes up.

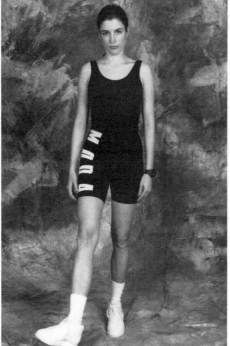

26. Now roll your ankle to the right.

27. Continue rolling your ankle towards the floor …

28. … and to the left …

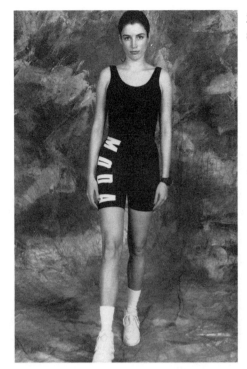

29. ... and back to the start.

KNEE BEND

30. Stand in an upright position with your feet about shoulder-width apart.

31. Gently bend your knees.

SKIER'S KNEE ROLL

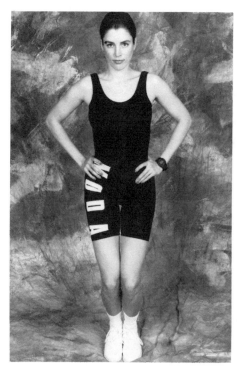

32. Stand in an upright position with your knees comfortably bent and your hands on your waist.

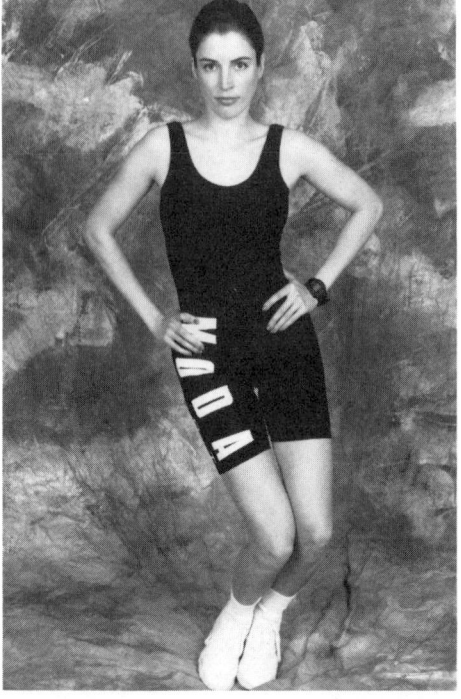

33. Roll your knees to the left …

34. … and then to the right.

CALF STRETCH

35. Stand in an upright position …

36. … and then step forward with your right leg to stretch your left calf. You control the amount of stretch by bending or straightening your right leg. Repeat the exercise with your other leg.

KNEE LIFT AND STRETCH

37. Stand in an upright position.

38. Lift your right leg and pull it to your chest with your arms.

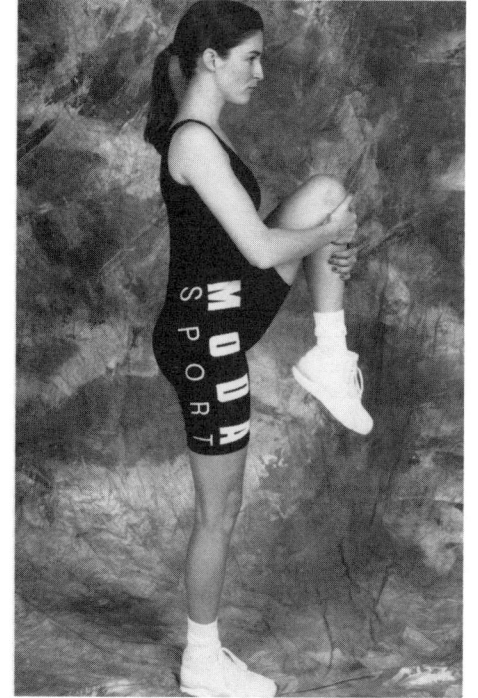

39. Repeat the exercise with your other leg.

UPPER LEG STRETCH

40. Raise your left leg and hold it with your left hand as shown.

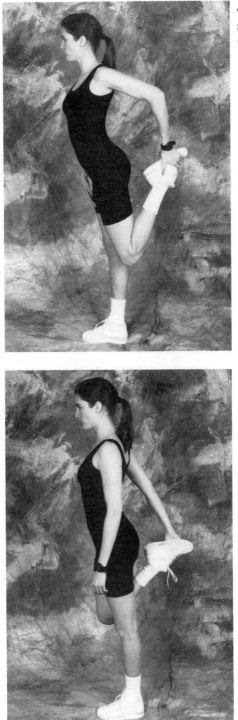

41. To achieve a greater stretch, pull the leg towards your body.

42. Switch legs.

43. Be careful not to strain your knee. It's also important not to let your shoulders "twist" around.

WALL SIT

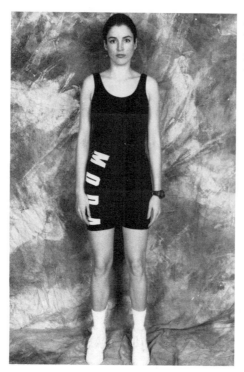

44. Stand with your back to a wall with your feet about shoulder-width apart.

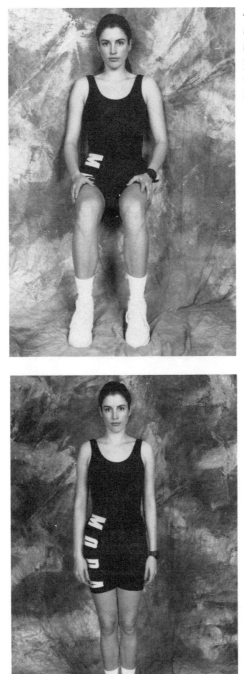

45. Place your back against the wall and slide down into a sitting position. This is excellent for strengthening your legs!

46. To make this exercise even harder, try it with your legs together.

47. See how long you can maintain this position. It's okay to rest your hands on your thighs, but don't apply any pressure to your knees by pushing against them with your hands.

INNER THIGH STRETCH

48. Stand with your feet apart and hands on your thighs as shown.

49. Straighten your left leg and bend your right leg as shown to stretch your inner thigh. Keep your feet pointed straight ahead.

50. Repeat the exercise on the other side of your body. Your upper body can be kept upright ... or you can lean forward onto your hands.

SKIER'S HOP

51. Stand as pictured … almost as though you were skiing down a hill!

52. Lift your left leg and "hop" to the side.

53. Land on your right leg and bring your feet together again. Now hop back to the other side. Repeat the exercise.

LEG STRETCH #1

54. Sit on the floor and hold your ankles as pictured.

55. Keeping your back straight, push your knees towards the floor with your elbows to stretch your inner thighs.

LEG STRETCH #2

56. Sit on the floor with your legs extended to the side as pictured. Don't overstretch—if you feel a "pulling" sensation, you're probably overdoing it.

57. Reach over your leg to stretch. For an advanced stretch, hold onto your ankle or foot.

58. Repeat the exercise on the other side of your body.

LEG STRETCH #3

59. Sit on the floor and pull your right leg into your groin while extending your left leg out to the side.

60. Lean over your knee and hold your ankle.

61. Repeat the exercise with your foot pointed ... and then on the other side of your body.

LEG STRETCH #4

62. Stand with legs a few feet apart and then bend left knee to lower yourself to the floor while keeping your right leg straight and flexed. The pictures show the maximum flex.

63. Now point your toes.

64. Stand up and lower yourself down on the other side and flex your foot.

65. Once again, point your toes.

LEG STRETCH #5

66. To get into the position pictured, step forward with your left leg as if walking ... then bend your left leg and reach for the floor.

67. Now lower your right knee to the ground and reach with your left hand to grab hold of your right foot.

68. Repeat the exercise with your other leg forward.

69. *Remember, if it hurts—don't force it!*

LEG LIFT #1

70. Kneel on ground as pictured, with weight evenly distributed.

71. Lift your right knee until it's parallel to the ground.

72. Repeat the exercise with your other leg.

73. It's important to keep your hips parallel to the ground ... don't let them rise up with your leg.

LEG LIFT #2

74. Lie on your right side with your knees slightly bent as shown.

75. Keeping your knees bent, raise your upper leg. Don't let your butt go backwards. Do the exercise on both sides of your body!

LEG LIFT #3

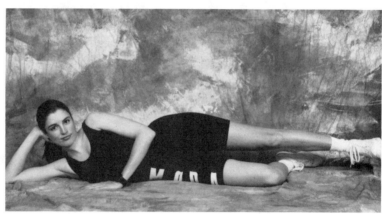

76. Lie on your right side as shown.

77. Lift your left leg into the air. Once again, don't "fall off" backwards.

78. For an advanced version of the same exercise, start with your leg in front of you as shown.

79. Raise your leg. It's not important to raise your leg very high. Repetition is the goal!

LEG LIFT #4

80. Lie on right side as shown. With left leg crossed in front of right, raise right leg off the ground a few inches. What keeps you balanced in these exercises is your front hand.

81. Now raise the leg into the air.

SIT-UPS #1

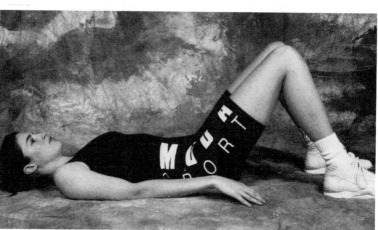

82. Lie on your back with your knees raised and your arms at your sides. Your feet should be slightly apart.

83. "Crunch" your stomach, look up, and reach forward with your arms. Don't let your head come too far forward since this can strain your neck.

84. For maximum effect, "crunch" farther forward.

SIT-UPS #2

85. Lie on your back with your hands behind your head. Now raise your knees as shown and cross your feet at the ankles.

86. "Crunch" your abdominal muscles and lift your head, neck, and shoulders off the floor. Don't let your chin touch your chest and be careful not to let your arms push your head too far forward.

BUTT LIFT

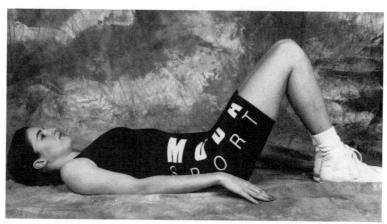

87. Lie on your back with your knees raised and your hands at your sides. Keep your knees and feet together to make the exercise hard … keep them slightly apart to make the exercise easier.

88. Raise your hips into the air as shown.

PUSH-UPS

89. To make the exercise easier, do the push-ups on your knees as shown. If this feels easy, then do them with your legs straight and toes on the ground.

90. Lower yourself to the ground as shown.

RELAXING STRETCH

91. Kneel on the floor as shown.

92. Start to lower yourself backwards ...

93. ... until you're all the way down. It's important to keep your arms stretched out in front of you.

4

Basic Skills

So now you think you are ready to jump on a chairlift and go charging up the slopes for your first skiing adventure! To help make sure your first adventure is a successful one, it is a very good idea to spend an hour or so learning the *basics* of maneuvering and getting around on skis *before* getting on any type of lift.

Practicing the skills presented in this chapter can be done on flat ground. Mastering these basic skills will help ease the initial frustration some skiers experience during the first few hours they spend wearing skis.

For example, before you can get on a chairlift, you're going to have to walk to the lift (with your skis on) ... and then maneuver yourself into the appropriate position to catch the chair. You may also have to "break" your forward movement as you slide around in the lift line—a very helpful skill to have mastered (or at least tried) before you even get into the lift line.

You will find that learning with *short skis* (150cm to 170cm) is a lot easier than learning with long skis. To speed up your learning process, you may want to start out on short skis. You can then slowly increase the length of the skis you use as your skill and comfort levels on skis increase.

When should you tackle your first hill? Well, once you feel comfortable and reasonably confident moving around on flat ground and have a basic understanding of a snowplow, you're ready to try your first hill. Just don't forget to have fun!

BASIC SKIING POSITION

1. This is your basic skiing position. Your weight is evenly distributed on each ski and you should stand upright with your knees bent comfortably forward. Your weight should be centered and slightly forward as you bend your knees. Hold your poles in front of your body at about waist level. You should feel relaxed, comfortable, and unstressed in this position.

WALKING WITH SKIS

Walking with skis is basically "pulling" yourself along with your poles.

2. Plant your right pole and prepare to pull your right leg forward.

3. As the right leg moves forward, reach forward and plant the left pole.

4. Continuing to walk forward, slide/pull the left leg forward, past the planted left pole, and prepare to plant the right pole.

SKATING WITH SKIS

Skating with your skis is another way of moving forward on flat ground. The technique is the same as skating with ice skates.

5. This skier has just pushed off with the right ski and is now "gliding" on the left ski.

6. The right ski is placed in front as she prepares to "push off" with her left ski.

7. After pushing off with the left ski, glide on the right ski.

GLIDING

Gliding after a pole push is another way to slide around flat ground. Skiers also resort to "push gliding" (and skating) when they start to lose speed in flat areas.

8. The skier has just pushed herself forward with her poles and is now gliding.

9. Planting both poles in front of her, she pulls herself forward.

10. Bending forward aids in achieving a strong pull/push.

11. Glide as far as you can after you push off with your poles.

HERRINGBONE WALK

The "herringbone" walk is used to walk uphill. The key to success is to roll your knees slightly inward so the inside edges of your skis can "grip" the snow.

Why would anyone want to walk uphill? The most common reason is to recover dropped equipment (such as a pole after a fall).

12. Using your poles (if you have them!) for support, face uphill.

13. Lift your right leg and move it up the hill.

14. Put your right leg down and prepare to lift your left leg.

If done vigorously, it's possible to walk uphill fairly fast in this manner.

SIDESTEPPING

Sidestepping is the way most people walk uphill. The key to success is to roll your knees slightly into the hill so your uphill edges "grip" the snow.

15. Stand across the hill so your skis aren't pointing uphill or downhill.

16. Using your downhill pole for support, lift your uphill leg.

17. Move it up the hill.

18. Lift your downhill leg and start to bring it uphill.

19. Bring the downhill leg alongside the uphill leg.

You can sidestep uphill in a "hopping" motion if you need to move fast.

SIDE SLIPPING

Side slipping is used to "slide" down something you don't want to—or can't—ski down. Skiers also side slip down a hill if they only want to move a few feet (such as when picking up a friend's dropped pole).

20. To hold your position on the hill, roll your knees uphill as this skier is doing. While her position is slightly exaggerated for the hill on which this picture was shot, it becomes critical on steep or icy slopes.

21. Note how the uphill edges of the skis are "gripping the snow." The purpose of the body position in the previous picture is to get your skis in this position while maintaining your balance.

22. To start your skis "slipping" downhill, roll your knees downhill until your skis are flat on the snow . . . at which point you'll start to slide downhill sideways.

23. This is the correct body position while side slipping down the hill.

24. To stop yourself from sliding, roll your skis back onto their edges. By alternating the position of your skis (on their edges or flat), you can control how fast your skis side slip down the hill.

KICK TURN

A kick turn is a means of doing a 180-degree turn without skiing forward. It's useful when you want to turn around without moving forward (as when the hill is too steep for your ability and you don't want to point your skis downhill).

25. Prepare to execute a kick turn by placing your poles as shown for support.

A WORD OF CAUTION: Executing a kick turn requires that your knees and legs be fairly flexible. If you have weak knees or legs, don't try this.

26. Lift your left leg forward and let the back of your ski rest on the ground.

27. Let your ski fall across your body ...

28. … until it comes to rest on the ground facing the opposite direction.

29. Move your poles for support and prepare to lift the other ski.

30. Lift your right leg and swing it across your body ...

31. ... until it comes to rest alongside the other ski. You're now ready to ski off in the new direction!

FALLING

All skiers experience the fear of being out of control at some point in their skiing career. As a novice, you're bound to feel out of control a lot during your first few hours on the slopes since you won't have mastered stopping!

32. Feeling her speed is out of control, this skier starts to sit back on her skis to make a controlled fall.

33. To fall "cleanly," she shifts her weight to the side ...

34. ... and lets herself slide into the ground. Note that the poles are held clear of the body.

35. After sliding a few feet, she comes to a stop. This type of fall is much safer than "hitting" something because you were out of control and didn't know how to stop.

The easiest way to stop if you feel out of control is simply to sit back on your skis and then fall to the side. You *should* fall in this manner anytime you are in danger of hitting someone or something.

GETTING UP

Okay ... now you're on the ground. How do you get up?

36. Bring your skis together across the hill; your skis should be downhill and your body should be uphill. You should also make sure that your skis are pointing *across* the hill or you'll start to slide as soon as you start to get up.

37. Sit up and hold your poles together as shown.

38. Start to push yourself up with your poles.

39. Continue to push yourself up with your poles …

40. ... until you come to a standing position.

SNOWPLOW

41. The snowplow is an easy way to stop and/or control your speed. In fact, even experienced skiers use the snowplow to control their speed at times. The skier in this photo has just gotten off a chairlift and is holding two pairs of poles. She also has undone some of the buckles on her right boot ... and she looks cold. At times like this, snowplowing (as she is doing) is the safest way to maintain control.

Another nice aspect about a snowplow stop is that it can be done in very little space. You can completely stop your forward motion without turning to the side at all— even if you're pointed straight downhill!

42. Ski in a straight line.

43. To get into the snowplow position, slide your heels apart and roll your knees inward to get on the inside edges of your skis.

44. To stop forward motion completely, apply more outward pressure with your heels. Note how this skier is "rolling" her knees inward to make maximum use of her inside edges.

45. Here's how the snowplow looks from the back.

5

The Skiing Environment

Now that you have an understanding of the basics of moving around on skis, you may want to familiarize yourself with the *skiing environment* before you go charging onto the slopes! Skiing has become much more comfortable in recent years, and one of the contributing factors is the many improvements that have been made around the skiing environment. Skiers in the 1960s, for the most part, had to endure rope tows, slow chairlifts, long lift lines, and poorly groomed and marked slopes. Conversely, most modern resorts feature fast chairlifts that are capable of transporting up to four skiers at a time ... the result being extremely short lift lines.

What follows is a description of some of the things you may encounter on a typical ski resort mountain.

SNOWCATS

A common sign on most mountains is "Beware Of Snowcats." A few years ago, after seeing one of these signs, my (then five-year-old) sister, Zuleika, asked, "What's a snowcat, Dad ... and how big do they get?" She was concerned about running into a snowcat. After all, if snowcats weren't dangerous predatory animals, why would they post "beware" signs?

Actually, snowcats are machines that groom the slopes, usually at night to minimize risk. However, you do need to be aware that maintenance equipment can be encountered on the slopes and that most of these machines aren't capable of maneuvering around you — meaning you must avoid them!

Some mountains offer night skiing, and extra precaution is advised to avoid a possible skier/machine encounter. Once while night skiing, Christine narrowly missed colliding with a ski mobile that was coming up the mountain with a broken headlight. A distance of about three feet and some fancy footwork were all that separated her from a possible injury!

NIGHT SKIING

Many mountains offer night skiing (at least for a few hours) during the peak seasons. One advantage is that the slopes are usually considerably less crowded at night. Also, if you work all day, night skiing may be your only opportunity to hit the slopes! Possible disadvantages are that it's usually colder at night and the slopes are often worn down from the day's use. The result is that you have to watch out for possible icy spots.

To enable skiers to see at night, bright lights are placed along the runs. Generally, fewer runs are open at night; although restaurants, ski school classes, and other facilities are usually open.

LIFTS

Walking up the mountain before you ski down is time-consuming and tiring. In fact, probably the invention most responsible for turning downhill skiing into a popular mainstream sport was the invention of the uphill "lift."

Lifts come in six forms ... actually seven if you include helicopter skiing!

Rope Tow

The *rope tow* was the first type of lift to be put into use. Usually, it was powered by an old automobile engine. Skiers simply held onto the rope and let it pull them up the hill. An early rope tow in Vermont was nicknamed "Suicide Six" after the six cylinder engine that powered the lift. The name was coined because the engine often broke down—making riding the lift a haphazard affair at best. The ski area "Suicide Six" is still in operation today.

The disadvantage to the rope tow is that skiers had to support their weight with their arms—a tiring proposition! On a steep hill, many skiers were so worn out by the time they reached the top that they wouldn't want to repeat the effort again.

Rope tows only exist today on extremely shallow "bunny hills" that are used almost exclusively for children.

To ride a poma lift, place the disk between your legs and let it pull you up the hill.

Poma Lift

A big improvement over the rope tow is the *poma lift*. Poma lifts are made up of a hanging rope with a round disk at the end. Skiers place the disk and rope between their legs and allow the lift to "pull" them up the hill. The skier still has to support his weight somewhat. Poma lifts also require that skiers pay attention while on the lift since they have to control the direction of their skis as they travel along the ground. For these reasons, poma lifts are usually only used on short slopes.

One consideration when using a poma lift is that the takeoff on some of them can be described as nothing short of being "launched" ... which is part of the fun of using them!

J-Bar

Also known as the "Yo Baby" bar (by some skiers), the *J-bar* is a "hook" shaped bar that skiers place behind themselves and are then pulled up the hill. A mistake many novice skiers make is attempting to "sit" on the bar—which you can't do since it won't support your weight. The trick is simply to stand upright and let the lift pull you up the hill. As with the poma lift, skiers have to control the direction of their skis.

T-Bar

The *T-bar* is capable of transporting two skiers at a time and is basically just a modified J-bar. Since the bar rests on your butt, the one thing you want to avoid is getting on the lift with a child or someone who is a lot shorter than you. If the bar is resting on an eight-year-old's butt, and you're on the chair with him ... the bar will most likely end up behind your knees! Not a pleasant way to be pulled up the hill! One option used by many instructors and parents is to hold the child in front of them between their legs.

T-bars are generally only used at small local mountains, since chairlifts are faster and more comfortable (but more expensive to install).

Chairlifts

The most frequently encountered type of lift is the *chairlift*. Chairlifts are described as being a "double chair" (which carries two skiers at a time), a "triple chair" (carries three skiers), or a "quad chair" (carries four). Although we haven't personally seen one, we hear some resorts now have chairs capable of carrying more than four skiers at a time.

Chairlifts have the advantage of allowing skiers to relax completely since they don't have to control their skis as they do when on a poma lift. All you do is sit in the chair and let it whisk you up the mountain. Most chairs even feature some type of foot rest!

Chairlifts have the added advantage of allowing you to get to know your fellow skiers. Since all chairlifts carry at least two people at a time, it's customary to yell out "single" when you arrive at the lift if you're alone. Besides possibly getting you to the front of the line where another single may be, you may also end up meeting an attractive member of the opposite sex! Paul's brother, for example, often abandons him in line to become a "single" if he hears or sees an attractive girl looking for a chair partner.

Since most chairs carry skiers high above the ground, you will have the opportunity to take in some spectacular scenery while riding the chair. Some skiers only decide which runs they will take after they have the opportunity to evaluate them from the bird's-eye view they get while riding the chair.

Keep in mind that some chairlift operators won't let you ride the lift if you have on any loose, long, or dangling pieces of clothing. They don't want you to be "hung" by a dangling scarf or other such item.

Occasionally chairlifts break down. Sometimes for a few moments — and sometimes for longer. If you should become stranded, don't jump, and make sure the safety bar is down since the chair may "lunge" unexpectedly when the lift starts up again. Rest assured that you will be rescued if need be. If you jump, you'll probably end up seriously injuring yourself.

Getting On and Off Chairlifts

The first few times you ride any type of lift, tell the lift operator that it's your first time. He'll most likely slow the lift down to help you get on and to give you more time to get in position. However, many lifts are automatically designed to move slowly while they pick up skiers.

To get on the chair, the procedure is as follows:

Look at the chair and figure out which side of your body the chair's "pole" will be on. A double chair, for example, will often be hanging from a pole that attaches in the center of the chair. The reason you need to take note of this is that you want to have both of your ski poles in the opposite hand so you can grab the chair's pole with your free hand. If you will be grabbing the chair with your right hand, you don't want to be holding your poles, gloves, or anything else on your right side when the chair arrives. Figuring all this out *before* it's your turn to "board" the chair will make your life simpler.

When you move into position to catch the chair, try not to let your ski tips cross. Look over your shoulder (on the side you will grab the support pole), hold both your ski poles in the other hand, and simply sit when the chair arrives.

Once you're clear of the loading area, put the safety bar down. You don't want to do a face plant from forty feet up in the air!

When you approach the unloading area, lift your ski tips up so they don't "catch" the front of the ramp and get pulled off. As soon as you can support your weight by standing up ... do so. Usually, there's a small hill (ten feet long or so) where you unload, which helps you get clear of the chair and the skiers in the next chair behind you.

Usually you will have the choice of skiing straight off the chair or skiing off to the left or right. If you are on the lift with another skier, it's a good idea to tell them what direction you're planning to go. If you don't, you may end up turning into each other as you unload.

Gondolas

Gondolas are capable of carrying a lot of skiers at once and often travel great distances in a short period of time. Generally, gondolas are more common in Europe than in the U.S. The disadvantage to gondolas is that they're a bit tedious since you have to take your skis off before you can ride in them. Also, there's usually only two gondolas on a line so you may have to wait for one a bit longer than you would for a chair.

Helicopters

One of the most exclusive ways to ski is to go "helicopter skiing." This is an activity best reserved for the advanced skier. However, if you want to ski fresh "virgin" powder, and have a bit of extra cash, then you may want to try one of the ultimate skiing adventures.

Helicopter skiing services transport skiers to powder bowls and other ultimate skiing spots on top of some of the best mountains in the world. The obvious advantage is that you'll be "making tracks" on snow that hasn't seen another pair of skis. Keep in mind, however, that this is an expert skier's activity. If you fall, the ski patrol won't be around to "snowmobile" you out!

HAZARDS ───────────────────────

"It says Haa-zards aren't marked," said Christine to a confused looking Val and Chipper. She was reading a posted sign at the top of a run we were about to take.

"What?" asked Val.

"It says that Haa-zards aren't marked," repeated Christine.

After a few moments of confusion, Val caught on. "You mean hazards aren't marked," replied Val, finally realizing what Christine meant. Being French, Christine had mispronounced the word. For the rest of the day we all yelled warnings whenever we saw a "haa-zard."

"Oh no, I've hit another haa-zard," yelled Val as he heard the grinding sound of a rock scraping a gouge in the bottom of his skis.

Actually, hazards are usually marked with sticks. Anytime you see a couple of sticks sticking in the snow, they are probably marking a rocky or bare spot. Do feel free to use the term "Haa-zards" if you wish!

OUT OF BOUNDS

"Out of bounds" refers to the areas of a mountain that aren't designated as public ski runs. To get into an out of bounds area, you must usually go under a rope that states that the other side is "Out Of Bounds."

The danger in skiing out of bounds is that the ski patrol doesn't check these areas. If you become injured, for instance, and can't ski or walk out, you could freeze to death.

THE SKI PATROL

Ski areas are patrolled by the "ski patrol." These individuals are easily identified by their common uniforms and are there to offer assistance to skiers in need. In fact, it often amazes us how quickly these people show up if you look the slightest bit troubled. Recently, while taking pictures for this book, Paul hiked up a hill under a chairlift in what seemed like a full-blown blizzard. He took off his skis and "hiked" because skiing down the cliff seemed like nothing short of suicidal due to the cliff's steepness and the near zero visibility. So he was amazed when a ski patrolman skied down the cliff as if it were a sunny afternoon and he was out for a relaxing run on the bunny hill.

"Are you all right?" asked the patrolman when he arrived at Paul's side. "I thought it was unusual to see someone standing out here without skis in this weather."

After Paul told him he was okay and was just taking pictures, he happily skied off as if skiing in these kinds of conditions—and in this kind of weather—was the most natural thing in the world.

The point is that the ski patrol is there to help you and make your skiing experience safer and more enjoyable.

SKILL LEVEL SIGNS

All slopes are marked with *slope skill level indicators*. These are: a green circle, a blue square, a black diamond, or a double black diamond.

The *Green Circle* is used to mark the *novice* slopes and is the easiest way down. Some green slopes can become so flat that it becomes necessary to "push" yourself along with your poles.

The *Blue Square* is used to mark slopes that are designated for the *intermediate* skier. Generally, these are the slopes that are the most common on mountains since the majority of recreation skiers fit into this category. Intermediate slopes can be steep or flat ... or they may be covered with bumpy moguls. In other words, almost any type of terrain may be encountered.

The fact that the "blue" runs get so much use also means that they can become icy towards the end of the day as skiers scrape the loose snow off ... so keep your eyes open!

The *Black Diamond* is used to mark slopes that require *expert* skill level to ski. These slopes may be extremely steep and bumpy, which you may consider fun if you have the ability to handle these types of conditions!

Double Black Diamond runs are a novice skier's nightmare. These slopes are unquestionably the toughest the mountain has to offer.

Remember that different mountains have different standards as to what an "expert" skier is or what an "intermediate" slope is. In other words, one mountain's black diamond runs may be the equivalent to another mountain's blue square runs. The moral of the story is to approach any new mountain with respect and caution.

OTHER SIGNS

Some other signs you should pay attention to are:

Slow. A "SLOW" sign is usually posted in areas where skiers converge from a couple of different directions, such as around a lodge where numerous runs may end. It's important to pay attention when skiing through these areas. On a recent ski trip we watched a skier changing the tape in his portable tape player while skiing along at thirty miles an-hour. The amazing thing was he was looking down at what he was doing rather than looking where he was going. So it wasn't surprising when he plowed into the back of an inexperienced skier and lifted her cleanly out of her boots—carrying her a good hundred feet down the hill before stopping. Fortunately, no one was hurt. Obviously it's in your own best interest to slow down when you see signs indicating such.

Emergency Phone. Emergency phones are usually marked with a large sign stating *Emergency Phone* and may also have the symbol of a phone in a red square. These phones can usually be found at various sites around the mountain.

Danger. The sign for danger on most mountains is a red exclamation mark in a triangle. Naturally, anytime you see this symbol you should slow down and pay attention.

Slope Closed. Occasionally, various slopes are closed due to poor snow conditions, maintenance work, accidents, and numerous other reasons. On most mountains, the symbol is a skier in a red circle with a line through it. Don't ski on slopes marked closed.

Nastar. A large "N" is often used to mark slopes that are being used for Nastar races. These slopes may be open to the public or may not. It's a good idea to check with the ski patrol since you won't win any popularity contests if you inadvertently ski onto an active race course!

Some signs at the bottom of the hill that you may want to look for are:

Tickets. Lift passes are often sold near the main chairs as well as inside the base lodge. By spotting the ticket outlet near the chair you may avoid a long walk into the lodge. Smaller mountains, however, may only have one ticket office.

Ski School. The ski school meeting places are generally marked with a picture of a *bell*. If you are scheduled for a lesson, you will most likely meet in one of these areas. If you're not in ski school, then you may want to avoid these areas since they often become crowded.

First Aid Facility. First aid clinics are marked with a "plus" sign; they are often identical in color to the plus signs on the back of the jackets worn by the ski patrol.

Restaurants. Lodges that offer food usually have a knife and fork symbol next to their locaiion on the trail maps.

Buses. Some ski areas are so big that it's possible to come off the mountain at a location that is a few miles away from where you started. On the trail maps of these resorts, "bus stops" are usually marked. You don't want to come down the mountain after the lifts close in an area that doesn't have transportation back to where you need to go!

Lifts Closed. Each lift has the time it stops running posted. This becomes important, for example, if you have to catch a certain lift to get back to the other side of the mountain at the end of the day.

TRAIL MAPS

Maps of the mountain are available where you buy your lift ticket; they're also permanently located at various sites around the mountain. These trail maps help you plan your day by identifying the skill level of each slope, as well as showing you where the lodges are located and other useful information. Carry a map with you; it will help you get the most out of the mountain.

LIFT TICKETS

Before you can ride on the various ski lifts, you'll need to buy a *lift ticket*. The tickets can be bought for a half day, a full day, three days, or a week. Some mountains offer a seemingly endless list of options, such as tickets that are good for six out of seven days (so you can rest one day). Check out all the options before you buy to be sure you get the type of ticket that best suits your needs. Some ski schools, for example, don't require you to have a lift ticket while you are in their classes.

You'll need to show your lift ticket almost every time you get on a lift, so be sure to attach it to your clothing in a convenient location. Personally, we don't like to have a lift ticket near our faces since the wind created by skiing fast can cause the ticket to "slap" you.

TYPES OF SNOW

As far as skiers are concerned, there are six types of snow that may be encountered and each requires a slightly different technique.

Hard Pack

This is the most common type of condition found on ski slopes ... it's also the type of snow you should initially learn to ski on. Hard pack is the result of slope grooming, and as its name implies, it is basically packed snow with very little powder on top. For the snow to remain hard, temperatures have to be fairly cool.

Slush

Slush describes what snow turns into when temperatures start to warm up. Naturally, "slushy" conditions are common at the end of the season. Slush is hard to ski because the wet snow is heavy, which makes controlling the direction of your skis difficult. Another problem encountered when skiing from hard pack onto slush unexpectedly is the sudden braking effect caused by the wet slush.

Falling in slush is definitely a wet experience!

Ice

At the other end of the temperature scale you may encounter icy conditions. In fact, at some east coast ski areas the slopes can become so icy that they look more like steep skating rinks than ski slopes! Skiing in these conditions requires more skill than skiing on soft snow. As far as novice skiers are concerned, it's probably best to try to avoid skiing on ice until they have mastered the basics.

Powder

For many skiers, skiing fresh powder is the ultimate experience! Powder is the term used to describe loose snow piled on the ground such as is found after a fresh snowfall. Once the powder has been groomed, it quickly becomes hard pack. For this reason true "powder hounds" like to hit the slopes in the early morning hours after a snowfall to make "fresh tracks"! Novice skiers can ski powder from day one as long as it's not more than a few inches deep. However, heavy powder conditions, such as when it's waist deep, are best left to the experts.

One advantage to skiing in powder is that falling becomes a very pleasant experience!

Crud

Crud, as its name implies, describes bad snow conditions and usually means loose, hard chunks of snow and ice. Loose powder that gets rained on and then freezes often results in "cruddy" conditions. Novice skiers should try to avoid skiing in crud.

Another type of crud comes in the form of a hard crust, usually the result of rain that has frozen on top of soft snow. Skiing on a crust isn't much fun since your skis usually break through the crust, creating a braking effect.

Manmade

Almost all ski resorts make snow sometime during their season by blowing a fine water mist in the air, which freezes and creates "snow." It is often described as "peanut butter" by experienced skiers due to the fact that manmade snow is slower to ski on than natural snow. The first time you ski from natural snow to manmade snow you'll probably be surprised by the breaking effect. However, manmade snow is better than no snow! We'd also rather ski on manmade snow than on rock-covered snow.

So, how do you know what conditions exist on the mountain? One source of information is at the bottom of the chairlifts where conditions are usually posted for the areas the chair services. Also, most ski areas have a phone-in ski report that tells skiers what conditions are like on the mountain. By skiing in conditions that match your skill level you'll help avoid having a possible bad experience.

A skier enjoys the wide open spaces of the "Big Burn" on Snowmass Mountain.

Skiing is an extremely social sport—and the lodge on the mountain is an excellent place to meet people while getting a tan!

Skiers are fun people to be around!

Sno-Zone hats are terrific because you can wear them as hats—or as full face masks if conditions are cold.

When it's snowing, it is important to wear goggles (instead of sunglasses).

Ski bindings should be easy to operate on the slopes. All skiers have to do to pop out of these Marker Bindings is push down the back of the binding with their ski pole.

Skiers usually see beautiful scenery while riding the chairlift.

Trail maps are posted on the mountain to aid skiers in selecting which runs they will ski. Foldup pocket versions are also available for free.

A quad chair is capable of transporting four skiers at a time.

Connecting your parallel turns is a fun way to ski and stay in control.

Top: This skier is sitting back on his skis to unweight them as he skis over the top of a pile of snow (soon to become a mogul). Center: After lightly jumping into the air, he lands and "edge sets" into the turn ... Bottom: ... and skis off in the new direction.

This "leash" is a unique way to keep track of your child on the slopes.

A junior skier takes a breather on the slopes.

6

Intermediate Skills

Now that you know how to snowplow, the next step is to learn a snowplow turn! However, before you learn any type of turn you should become familiar with the concept of the *fall line*.

The fall line is simply the steepest line down the mountain. If you ski into the fall line, *your speed will increase*. As you turn away from the fall line, *your speed will decrease*. This becomes important because when you turn, you ski across the fall line. At some point during your turn, your skis will be pointing straight downhill, or down the fall line. It's important to keep turning past this point or you'll pick up speed very quickly!

ALWAYS FINISH YOUR TURNS

VERY IMPORTANT: *Always finish your turns*! More than anything else you can do, finishing your turns is the most important technique you can use to control your speed. As you begin to ski steeper hills, this becomes even more critical. If you don't finish your turns, you will always be skiing down the fall line and you won't be able to "check" your speed. Remember, the only way to slow down, or stop, is to get your skis across the hill. Many skiers don't seem to understand this — the result being they're always out of control!

UNWEIGHTING

To unweight your skis is to "unstick" them momentarily from the snow so that you can change direction with the least amount of resistance possible. For example, you must unweight your skis when you begin a parallel turn.

How do you unweight your skis? By quickly standing

up. The natural skiing stance has bent knees, so to un-weight your skis all you have to do is stand up. At the moment you become upright, your skis will be unweighted.

Another way some skiers unweight their ski is to "sit" suddenly. By sitting down, their knees are pulled up, which unweights their skis. This type of unweighting is often used when skiing moguls because skiers often have to bend their knees to "absorb" the bumps.

EDGING YOUR SKIS

To *edge your skis* is to put pressure on the metal edge that runs along the bottom of each side of your skis. You put your skis on edge by rolling your knees in the direction you want to edge (see photo #7 in this chapter for a detailed look). "Edging" your skis serves two purposes:

First, *you turn skis by edging them.* A more detailed description of how to do this will be discussed later. For now, it's important you understand the concept of "edging" your skis.

Second, *you prevent slipping downhill by edging your skis.* On a steep hill you must edge your skis into the hill to keep from sliding … even when standing still. A good example of this is when you want to stop side slipping, as discussed in Chapter 4.

SNOWPLOW TURN

1. The skier plants her pole in preparation for the turn. It should be noted that a *snowplow* turn can be made with or without the use of poles.

2. What makes you turn is applying weight to the inside edge of your outside ski . . . which is what this skier is doing as she prepares to turn around her pole. The "outside" ski refers to the ski that is uphill prior to starting the turn. At the end of the turn, the "outside" ski will be downhill. In this picture, the skier's right ski is the outside ski.

3. Continuing to apply pressure to the outside ski, the skier continues the turn. During the turn, almost no weight is put on the inside ski (left leg in this photo); it simply "follows" along. This is the point in the turn when you may feel a little panicky because your skis are pointing straight downhill. The thing to remember is to keep pressure on your outside ski and to *finish your turn*.

4. Keeping pressure on the outside ski, the skier continues the turn. Note the position of the poles.

5. Once you have finished your turn, you should again evenly distribute your weight on both your skis.

TRAVERSING

To *traverse the hill* means simply to ski from one side to the other. If, for example, you were on a hill that was too difficult for you to ski, you could "traverse the hill" ... slowly coming down while traversing from one side to the other. At the end of each traverse you could execute a "kick turn" or a controlled "skiing" turn such as a snowplow turn. In other words, you can traverse a hill anytime you feel a more direct descent is beyond your comfort or skill level.

Some skiers traverse a hill to get the most "mileage" from each run. Traversing is also an excellent way to control your speed until your ability increases to the point at which you can ski more directly down the fall line.

6. A skier traverses the hill. Note the body position.

7. When traversing steep or icy hills, it's important to "roll" your edges into the hill so that they hold your position without sliding sideways.

STEM CHRISTIE TURN

A *stem christie turn* is a transition turn between the snowplow turn and parallel turn. Once you are comfortable executing a snowplow turn, you should graduate to the stem christie.

8. Ski with your skis parallel. Look ahead and plan where you want to make your turn.

9. Slide your uphill ski (left leg in this photo) into a snowplow position and apply pressure to the ski's inside edge to initiate the turn.

10. Continue to apply pressure to the outside ski to keep turning.

11. At this point the turn is finished. The next step is to bring your skis parallel to each other as in Picture 8.

PARALLEL TURN

This is the most efficient way to turn your skis because you don't lose much speed during the turn.

12. In preparation to turn, the skier is about to plant her pole.

13. Moments after planting her pole, the skier has also unweighted her skis by raising her body upwards. To initiate the turn, she has transferred her weight to the outside (left) ski, applying pressure to the ski's inside edge. Note how the inside ski is completely unweighted and off the ground as it "follows" the outside ski. Lifting the inside ski is not necessary and is only done here for demonstration purposes.

14. Keeping pressure on the outside ski, the skier carves her turn. At this point in the turn the skis are pointing directly downhill. It's important to control your speed by *finishing your turn*!

15. Past the fall line, the skier finishes her turn.

16. As you come out of the turn, redistribute your weight evenly on each ski.

THE CHECK

Prior to turning, it's a good idea to "*check*" your speed. You can do this by dropping your weight and thrusting your heels slightly downhill as if you were going to stop—except you don't, you just turn uphill a bit to slow down a little before going into your turn. Doing a check before turning serves two functions: first, it *slows you down enough* to help you maintain control in the turn. And second, it *drops your weight* so you can then unweight as you go into the turn. Performing a check involves bending your knees, which puts you in a perfect position to stand up and unweight your skis as you begin your parallel turn.

CONNECTING YOUR PARALLEL TURNS

One of the things that makes a skier look good is the ability to connect parallel turns one after the other. It also keeps your speed under control, which is extremely important. Most skiers make a few turns, get into trouble, and then "bomb" down the rest of the hill almost, if not completely, out of control. Two important features in connecting your turns are:

Plan your line. Rather than simply taking off down the hill and skiing it "as it comes," look down the hill and try to visualize a few turns ahead. This way you'll see, and thus avoid trouble spots before you hit them (remember the hazards from Chapter 5?). Planning your route (or "line" in ski terminology) is an important step in connecting your turns.

Rhythm. Try to "feel" a rhythm as you make the transition from one turn to another. Some skiers ski with a portable tape player or radio (although these have been banned at some resorts) to help them ski in rhythm. Developing a continuing rhythm as you unweight and edge your skis will help you "flow" from one turn to another.

PARALLEL (OR HOCKEY) STOP

While snowplowing to stop works well at slow speeds, it doesn't work well if you're traveling fast. For this reason, most skiers use the *parallel* stop, which can be done from extremely high speeds. The key to success is to *use your edges* when you're "sliding" rather than letting your skis ride flat on the snow. If you don't get on your edges, you may slide down the hill indefinitely!

17. Ski in a straight line with your skis parallel. To prepare to stop, stand up to "unweight" your skis.

18. While your skis are unweighted, rotate your heels aggressively downhill to bring your skis across the hill. At the same time, "edge" your skis to create the braking effect. Note the skier's upper body position hasn't really changed as she transitions from skiing to stopping. Your upper body should point downhill the entire time.

19. To keep your skis on edge, you must roll your knees into the hill. Hold the position until you come to a complete stop.

7

Advanced Skills

One the things that separates advanced and expert skiers from skiers of less skill is the ability to handle a wide range of snow conditions. Different types of conditions require slightly different techniques. Three of the more common types of conditions you may encounter are:

Ice: Skiing on ice requires a much "quieter" style of skiing than most skiers are used to. Unweighting your skis prior to turning isn't really necessary since ice doesn't "hold" your skis the way sticky snow does. *You must use your edges when skiing on ice* since they're all that is preventing you from sliding down the hill! As you begin your turn, bend forward and roll onto your edges as early as possible. Pretend that you are skiing on thin "lake ice" that will break if you are too aggressive. What you don't want to do is "skid" your edges out by overturning. It's also important to keep moving from edge to edge. The goal is to be always *lightly* carving your turns.

The other important factor when skiing on ice is your *body position.* If you find yourself constantly slide slipping down the hill because your edges aren't holding, you're probably not rolling your knees into the hill enough. Remember, you'll have to *lean your upper body downhill to counterbalance rolling your knees uphill.*

Powder: On the opposite end of the snow conditions spectrum is powder. Skiing powder requires that you ski close to the fall — and ski fairly fast to keep your skis "planing." The concept is identical to water skiing in that you need speed to get "up on a plane." If you ski powder slowly, you'll "bog down" in the heavy snow and won't have the momentum to turn your skis.

Like a water skier, one way you can ski powder is to make "banked" turns. The technique can be practiced on hard pack first to get the hang of it. Simply (lightly) transfer your weight to the inside edge of the outside ski and go into a banked turn. As you come out of the turn, immediately start a banked turn in the other direction.

Remember, *when skiing deep powder you must ski close to the fall line to maintain your speed.* Traversing doesn't work in deep powder so you shouldn't attempt to ski it until you are fairly competent at connecting your parallel turns in a continuous rhythm.

Another technique used by most powder skiers is to keep their weight centered and their skis flat. The idea is not to "edge" too much and to "swing" your skis smoothly into the turn. Once again, speed is an important factor to enable you to overcome the weight of the snow.

Moguls: Skiing moguls requires strong legs and quick reflexes. It's also important to ski primarily from the waist down and to keep your upper body "quiet" and facing downhill. Skiing moguls requires that you plan ahead to avoid hitting an unexpected "jump" that may throw you off balance!

Think of your legs as shock absorbers and try to bend your knees to absorb bumps as you hit them. Our friend Bernard is an expert mogul skier and says the secret to success is to keep your upper body level—and to let your legs do all the work.

Another technique that works well in moguls is to unweight your skis by "sitting" down. As you ski into a mogul, bend your knees to absorb it; the upward motion of your knees unweights your skis. As your tips fly off the top of the mogul, swing your skis into the turn. As soon as you "land," do an edge set to check your speed. This type of turn is called a *Jet Turn* and works well in large moguls.

SPEED

Ironically, after years of working at edging their skis to maintain control, expert skiers begin to work at keeping their skis absolutely flat on the snow to ski as fast as possible. The minute you begin to edge your skis, you start to slow down. Now before you "bomb" down the nearest hill with your skis flat on the snow, realize that "downhilling" should only be done by skiers who have the control and ability to handle the excessive speeds.

On the other hand, you should start to become comfortable with a certain amount of speed in order to ski the types of conditions mentioned above. The best way is to try skiing fast under the guidance of an instructor.

The point is, speed is a part of becoming an expert skier.

JUMPING

The first time you *jump* while skiing, it will probably happen by accident. However, once you experience the thrill of flying through the air, you'll most likely start to jump off small bumps in the snow at every given opportunity! And if you get into downhill racing, then jumping will become an important part of your skiing repertory.

How to Jump

As you approach your takeoff, bend your knees and prepare to spring into the air. When you reach the jump, plant your poles in front of you where you anticipate leaving the ground.

When you reach the takeoff, stand up fast just before you leave the ground and "spring" into the air. You can also use your poles to "push off" if you are skiing slowly. It's important not to let your skis take off in front of you. If you jump late, your body may get left behind — which can throw you backwards and off balance.

As you rise into the air, lift your feet under your body. Think of it as tucking your heels under your butt. This position lines up your skis parallel with the hill; hold your poles low.

As you approach your landing, straighten your body and raise your arms out to your sides.

When you land, bend your knees to absorb the impact and keep the landing. If you time it just right, the *landing should be gentle and non-jarring*.

Keep in mind that JUMPING IS A HIGH RISK ACTIVITY and should only be attempted after you have become a competent skier. Also, don't approach your first few jumps at high speed or you may find yourself much higher in the air than you ever planned on being!

TAKE MORE LESSONS

One of greatest things you can do to improve your skiing is to take more lessons. Regardless of how well you ski, you can always improve your technique in some area. All the great skiers we know have spent a considerable amount of time in class. The mistake many skiers make is that they stop taking classes once they feel they're relatively under control on the mountain. Usually, they reach a plateau and don't progress much beyond it. If you want to become a great skier, take a few lessons each season!

8

First Aid

Sliding down a steep, slippery hill with a pair of six-foot-long planks bound to your feet is a potentially dangerous activity! Fortunately, injuries are fairly uncommon relative to the number of people involved in the sport ... and the odds of you needing to administer any type of first aid on the ski slopes are pretty slim. Even if an accident were to happen, ski patrol personnel are usually quick to respond to a victim's needs.

However, what would you do if you or a companion should become injured on the slope or be in need of assistance? What follows is some basic information that may help if you or a companion are unfortunate enough to become injured.

The following information is only presented to familiarize you with the concepts of first aid and should not take the place of certified instruction. In addition to reading the following text, you should also enroll in a first-aid class such as the one offered by the American Red Cross.

CROSS YOUR SKIS

Planting your skis in the snow so that they form an "X" is universally accepted to mean that help is needed. The "X" serves two functions: One, it alerts rescue personnel that you are in need of assistance, and two, it marks your location and helps prevent other skiers from accidentally skiing into the injured person, who may be hard to see while lying in the snow. In most cases, help will arrive almost immediately after you fall. Usually other skiers will stop and ask if assistance is needed when they see you have fallen and aren't getting up ... or if they see you have placed your skis (or someone else's) in the snow in an "X".

Generally, the best procedure is to ask the first skier

who stops to ski down the mountain and immediately alert the ski patrol that you or the victim is in need of assistance and is incapable of skiing down the mountain. Then wait with the victim until help arrives. If no other skiers are in the vicinity, you will have to go for help and leave the victim on the hill. Before leaving, there are three things you must do:

1. YOU MUST INSURE THAT THE VICTIM'S LIFE IS NOT IN IMMEDIATE DANGER. Life-threatening injuries such as severe bleeding, shock, and respiratory or heart failure must obviously be dealt with before you go for help.

2. MAKE SURE THE VICTIM IS OUT OF HARM'S WAY. If, for example, your companion has been injured by a collision with another skier due to poor visibility, you should try to insure that another collision won't take place while you are absent.

3. HELP IDENTIFY THE VICTIM'S LOCATION TO RESCUE PERSONNEL BY MARKING THE VICTIM'S LOCATION WITH CROSSED SKIS. If need be, you can also leave colorful clothing on the ground or in a nearby tree.

Emergency phones can be found in convenient locations at most resorts.

The ski patrol is well equipped to handle accidents should they happen.

STAY WITH THE VICTIM

If you don't have to leave the victim—don't. You can offer more aid and comfort by staying at your companion's side. Considering how crowded most ski slopes are, it's extremely unlikely you will have to leave the victim to go for help. Most ski resorts are patrolled by emergency personnel who usually are at a victim's side within minutes of an accident. The emergency personnel, commonly referred to as the "ski patrol," can usually be identified by the large red "plus" signs on the back of their jackets.

Obviously this is assuming you are wise enough not to ski in areas marked "Out Of Bounds." If you do ski in areas that aren't frequented by other skiers (such as extremely advanced runs or isolated powder bowls), you should consider carrying some type of signaling device such as a walkie-talkie, a whistle, an air horn, or some other type of device.

TREATMENTS

In an emergency, a basic knowledge of first aid may make the difference between life and death. Your primary goal is to stabilize the victim until rescue personnel arrive and take over. Although it's unlikely at a ski resort that has a ski patrol, you may also have to transport the victim off the mountain.

Treating most injuries isn't difficult; the key is to know what to do. To prepare properly, you may want to take one of the excellent first-aid courses offered through the American Red Cross. Following are some of the possible injuries you may encounter on the slopes.

Severe Bleeding

Severe bleeding must be halted immediately since the victim will become unconscious and die if blood loss is not stopped. The recommended course of action is:

Apply direct pressure. Ideally, a large compress should be pushed against the wound to stop the bleeding. In an emergency, you can apply direct pressure with your bare hands if nothing else is available.

A cloth works well because it absorbs the blood and allows it to clot. Once you have placed a compress over the wound, do not remove it as this may start the bleeding again. Leave it in place and let rescue personnel remove it at the hospital.

Direct pressure can also be applied by wrapping a shirt or similar type dressing around the wound. This is often ideal for cuts on the arms or legs.

Elevate the wound. Elevating the injured part of the body above the victim's heart helps retard bleeding due to gravity. Generally, cuts on the arms and legs can be easily elevated. One point to keep in mind is that you don't want to move or elevate any part of the victim's body if you suspect there might be a fracture. While it's still important to stop any bleeding, you don't want to create further damage by moving a broken limb before you put a splint on it.

Use pressure points. Another way to stop bleeding is to apply pressure on the main artery above the wound. Since this usually cuts off blood circulation to the entire limb, you should only use this technique if direct pressure to the wound and/or elevating the injured part of the body do not work. If you do stop the bleeding by using a pressure point, then try to alternate direct pressure over the wound with "point pressure." You don't want to cut off blood flow to the rest of the limb any longer than you have to.

Tourniquet. Applying a tourniquet should only be done if: (a) all of the above methods have failed; (b) the victim's life is in danger; and (c) there is no other course of action. TOURNIQUETS ARE EXTREMELY DANGEROUS AND

CAN CAUSE THE VICTIM TO LOSE THE LIMB. Generally, only extremely life-threatening injuries such as a severed limb will merit the use of a tourniquet. For further information about the use of tourniquets, enroll in a general first-aid course.

Frostbite

Frostbite is injury to body tissue by exposure to extreme cold. Frostbite can be a threat to a skier's nose, ears, and face since these areas are often exposed to the cold while skiing (although any part of the body that's exposed to the cold can develop frostbite). "Wind chill"—created by skiing fast—can freeze a skier's face (without him or her knowing it) in a relatively short period of time. For this reason, it's a good idea to ski on cold days with some type of face mask such as the ones made by Sno Zone.

The early symptoms of frostbite are "red looking" skin and painfully cold skin (often associated with wind chill). If the skier doesn't take action at this point to prevent frostbite, such as going indoors or putting on a face mask, gloves, or whatever is needed, the skin will change color as it freezes and become grayish yellow and/or white and feel extremely cold to the touch (although the victim may be too cold to feel it).

Advanced symptoms of frostbite are mental confusion, loss of eyesight, and death.

To treat frostbite, get the person indoors and warm the affected areas by placing them in warm (about 102 degrees F.) water. *Do not put the affected area in hot water. Don't rub the affected area to warm it since this could do further tissue damage.*

If water isn't available or you're forced to remain outdoors, wrap the victim in warm clothes or blankets and keep him as warm as possible. Don't, however, apply direct heat (such as a hot water bottle).

You should give the victim warm (not hot) liquids. *Do not allow the victim to drink alcohol* since alcohol is a vasoconstrictor and will hinder blood flow to cold body parts.

Watch the victim: it may be necessary to administer CPR if he stops breathing. As soon as possible, arrange to have the victim transported to a medical facility.

One of the dangers of frostbite is the fact that *once it has developed, there usually isn't any pain.* For this reason, it's extremely important that you take corrective action as soon as you feel cold, especially when your face, hands, feet, ears, and neck are cold. Some skiers, for example, ignore the fact that their nose is cold and forget about it when it "stops hurting," which ironically may indicate that frostbite has set in.

Hypothermia

Hypothermia is lower than normal body temperature. Hypothermia is a threat to skiers who allow themselves to become "chilled" when skiing ... and don't do something about it! Early symptoms are shivering, goosebumps, and feeling cold. Shivering occurs when the body tries to generate heat by forcing muscles to rub together.

If skiers develop any of these symptoms, they should take action and get out of the cold. If left untreated, advanced symptoms include mental confusion, "drowsiness," weakness, vasoconstriction (blood vessels narrow, and the blood withdraws to the center of the body to supply warmth to vital organs), shock, and eventually death. Naturally, frostbite is also a potential hazard to a skier who is experiencing hypothermia.

Treating hypothermia involves getting the victim warm, which for a skier with mild symptoms may simply mean going indoors as soon as she feels cold.

Additional treatment is the same as described for frostbite: Keep the victim warm, don't use extreme heat sources, treat for shock, give CPR if necessary, administer warm liquids, and arrange for transportation to a medical facility as soon as possible.

Fractures

A fracture is a broken or cracked bone; fractures can be generally grouped into two categories:

An *open fracture* is when part of the broken bone breaks the skin. You may or may not actually see the bone protruding from the body; in many instances the bone will break the skin during the accident and then slip back immediately afterwards. Even if the bone isn't visible, this type of injury is still an open fracture since an "opening" into the body has been made by the fractured bone. There's a high danger of infection whenever the skin is broken by bone fracture.

A *closed fracture* is a broken or cracked bone that doesn't break the skin. Most fractures associated with skiing are closed fractures.

Symptoms of a closed fracture include pain, discoloration, and swelling. The patient may also have heard the bone break or may feel the fractured bone parts "grating" as they rub together. You may see an obvious malformation that could only be the result of a broken bone.

If a fracture is suspected, don't move the victim until emergency personnel have arrived. As previously stated, it's highly unlikely you'll have to improvise a splint on the slopes since the ski patrol will probably be on the scene in a matter of minutes.

SPLINTS

However, should you have to move the victim before help arrives, you must first put a *splint* in place to prevent the fracture from moving. The following information is only presented to give you an understanding of the concepts involved; it is not intended to replace hands-on practice and instruction such as is available in a general first-aid class.

The objective of a splint is to prevent the fractured part of the body from moving. In an outdoor emergency in the snow, where there may be nothing to make a splint from, you can immobilize the injured part of the body by tying it to another part of the body. A broken leg, for example, can be bound to the victim's non-broken leg. A broken arm can be tied to the victim's chest. Keep in mind, however, that binding a fractured part of the body in this manner should only be done if there's positively no other way to form a splint.

Don't try to "straighten out" a fractured arm or leg before immobilizing it—you may create further damage. Try to immobilize the fractured part of the body in the position it's in.

In the case of an open fracture, you may also have to stop bleeding. Don't probe or try to push protruding bones back into the body. If there is a piece of bone protruding, wrap the entire wound in the cleanest cloth you have available. If any bone splinters have broken off or break off— don't attempt to put them back into the body. Keep the bone splinters loosely wrapped in a moist cloth for possible use by the orthopedic surgeon.

Splints can be made from folded blankets, folded jackets, parkas, and other types of clothing, ski poles (which can be broken to length), pieces of wood, and even skis. Keep in mind that we're talking about a "no alternative" type situation in the snow. In a more civilized environment, you would probably be able to find much more suitable materials.

Splints can be fastened in place with torn pieces of

clothing, belts, ski pole straps, handkerchiefs, bandanas, and other items that you may be able to improvise. Carrying a small pocketknife with you when you ski is a good idea in case you encounter an emergency.

The splint should be long enough to immobilize the joints on either side of the fracture. Place some padding between the splint and the patient's body to prevent pain. Remember, the primary objective of a splint is to *immobilize* the fracture.

Once the splint is in place, check periodically to see if it is cutting off the patient's circulation. If he loses feeling in his hands or feet, for example, or the injured area starts to swell or change color, then you may have to loosen the splint ties.

Special note: Fractures of the back and neck are extremely dangerous since even the slightest movement may cause damage to the spinal cord (which could cause paralysis). Even more so than the above mentioned injures, do not attempt to administer treatment yourself if there is any way to contact emergency personal.

If any type of back, neck, or head injury is suspected—even if the ski patrol is only a few moments away—*do not let the patient move, especially the head, neck, and back.*

Dislocations and Sprains

A *dislocation*, as its name implies, is a bone that has "dislocated" from a joint (such as a finger). A *sprain* is a torn or an overstretched muscle, tendon, or ligament. Differentiating between a fracture, a dislocated joint, and a sprain can be tricky. The best procedure is to get an X-ray.

Symptoms of dislocated joints and sprains include: pain, swelling, discoloration, and in the case of a dislocation, sometimes deformity.

Treating a dislocated joint is the same as a fracture—immobilize the joint. In fact, in the field you probably won't be sure if you're dealing with a closed fracture, a dislocation, or both.

Sprains are treated with cold compresses, rest, and elevating the injured area. Don't walk on a sprained ankle; you may damage it further. You should also remove your shoes and elevate your feet since foot swelling almost always accompanies a sprained ankle.

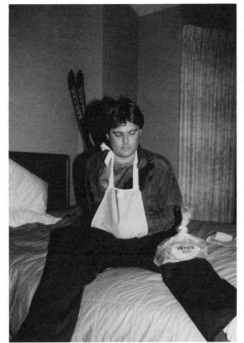

If you sprain or "pull" something, put ice on it to stop swelling. You may also have to immobilize the injured area with a sling.

Bruises

For some skiers, bruises are a fairly common occurrence; especially if you ski on ice and fall a lot! Symptoms include stationary pain, discoloration, swelling, pain from movement, and pain when pressure is applied.

Treatment should be rest and a cold compress to reduce swelling and rest.

Shock

Shock is a condition brought on when the body's vital organs are in a depressed state and/or the body's circulatory system is in a state of collapse. An accident victim can die from shock even if his or her initial injuries weren't necessarily threatening.

Symptoms of shock include: pale and/or clammy skin (a result of vasoconstriction), faint pulse, rapid pulse, decrease in blood pressure, irregular breathing (usually rapid and shallow), dilated pupils, and sometimes decreased kidney function. If left untreated, the victim may become unconscious and die.

To treat shock, give first aid to any injuries that may be the cause (such as an open wound with severe bleeding). Keep the victim calm and lying down. A patient's apprehension about what is happening can accelerate a state of shock. Talk to her and reassure her that she's going to be all right. Keep the victim warm and in a position that will best aid circulation. Usually the type of injuries sustained will dictate body position. If possible, have the injured person lie flat on her back. Give nonalcoholic liquids if the victim is calm and medical attention isn't nearby. Some injuries, such as ones that may allow fluids into the lungs, can be complicated by administering liquids.

Eye Injuries

Foreign matter in the eye can be highly annoying and may cause permanent damage if left untreated. When most people get "something in their eye," they complicate the condition by "rubbing" it. Don't rub your eye; you may do further damage by scratching the tender tissues.

To remove an object from the lower eye, gently pull down the lower eyelid while the patient looks up, and look for the source of the irritation. If you see an object, *gently* remove it with the corner of a piece of moistened tissue. Don't use dry cotton on or around the eye.

To remove an object from the upper eye, grasp the upper eyelid while the victim looks down. Pull the upper eyelid downward and slight outwards so it covers the lower eyelash, then release it and let the lower lid "scrape" the object off.

If the object is still in the upper eye, you can lift the eyelid upward while holding a match, or any similarly sized object, against the skin (*do not touch the eyeball or the inside of the eyelid with the match*). The idea is to lift the eyelid "around" the match so you can inspect the inside surface. If you see any foreign matter, gently remove it with the corner of a tissue.

If you should encounter an eye injury that involves the eye being penetrated by a foreign object, loosely bandage both eyes (you don't want to press against the eyes). Don't attempt to remove whatever has penetrated the eye as you may cause further damage. You must get the victim to an emergency eye specialist immediately.

Treat injuries around the eye for severe bleeding if need be, but avoid pressing against the eye.

Cardiopulmonary Resuscitation (CPR)

It's extremely important that you become proficient at performing *CPR* if you want to be adequately prepared to handle emergency rescue situations. The American Red

Cross, in addition to other agencies, offers excellent classes.

ACCIDENT MANAGEMENT

What action you take in the initial moments after an accident can dictate how effective your first aid and rescue will be. Some concepts to keep in mind are:

Keep calm. It's important that you keep calm, even if you are scared or frightened by the severity of the injury the victim has sustained. If an injured person sees that you are frightened by the sight of the injuries, he may go into shock from anxiety. Also, you may make a mistake and complicate the situation if you rush into action without thinking clearly.

Assess the situation. Don't leap into action without first making an assessment of what's wrong. While it is important to take action quickly to halt life-threatening conditions such as severe bleeding, you don't want to complicate matters either (such as by moving someone with a broken back). If the victim is conscious, listen to him; he can tell you what hurts and supply you with valuable information. Obviously, if the victim is in *immediate* danger (such as from an avalanche) you will have to move into action as soon as you arrive.

Evaluate the victim's breathing and heart rate. If the victim isn't breathing, you must take action at once to prevent loss of life.

Treat the most serious injuries first. After you assess the situation and have determined that the patient is breathing, treat the most serious injuries first. Your primary objective is to *stabilize* the victim until rescue personnel arrive.

FIRST-AID KIT

If you want to be well prepared in the event you encounter an accident on the slopes, you may want to carry a small first-aid kid in a waist pouch. Some items to carry are:

1. A small *pocketknife* to cut clothing and bandages. You may also opt for a pair of the blunt scissors that are specifically designed for this purpose. Make sure the points of sharp instruments are protectively "covered" so they don't puncture through the kit container and stab you (when you fall, for example).

2. *Absorbent gauze* to aid in stopping bleeding.

3. Four-inch *compress* to aid in stopping bleeding and to use as a dressing.

4. A rolled *gauze bandage* to use as a dressing.

5. A small *roll of tape* to hold dressings in place and to help hold splints in place.

Carrying more than the above mentioned articles really isn't practical or necessary since most ski patrols are extremely well prepared.

9

The Skiing Vacation

For many families, the words "skiing" and "vacation" mean the same thing. If you live in Florida or southern California, it may be impractical to travel to a "local" mountain due to the distances involved. Actually, ski resorts offer the most organized family vacation of any type of "specialty" sport. A scuba diving vacation, for example, may involve traveling to a distant island where non-diving family members will have little to do except watch your bubbles! Most ski resorts offer an endless variety of activities in addition to skiing. Aspen Village, in Colorado, offers vacationers hot air ballooning, horseback riding, ice skating, sledding, swimming, world-class dining, and a seemingly endless variety of shops … not to mention world-class skiing!

Considering the amount of money you may spend on a ski vacation, it's a good idea to do a little research before making your travel plans. Some of the things you should consider are:

Type and location of lodging. One of the most important considerations when selecting a hotel or condo is where it's *located* in relation to the mountain. Many skiers prefer accommodations that are actually located on the ski slope uphill of the lifts. This is ideal if you don't want to have to walk or travel far in your ski boots. Conversely, if being as close as possible to shops, restaurants, and other facilities is your primary concern, you may wish to seek accommodations in the center of town. The point is, don't assume that just because a hotel is "in the resort" it is conveniently located.

Another consideration is the *type* of accommodation. If you travel with a large group, you may prefer a condo instead of a hotel room. Condominiums often have kitchens, additional bedrooms, and "common areas" such as living and dining rooms, and are ideal for large families. Hotels, on

Traveling in a group is fun. It also helps cut down on cost since most resorts offer group packages at a discount.

the other hand, often offer vacationers restaurants, stores, room service, and other conveniences.

Size of the mountain and resort. Large mountains offer seemingly limitless ski trails, a large resort community, and a wide selection of conditions. Generally, skiers of all levels will find something to please them. Small mountains, on the other hand, are generally not as crowded as the bigger resorts. They're also often less expensive and thus may be ideally suited to your needs if your budget is tight. Another advantage to the smaller resorts is that they are often easier to get to since they are usually closer to cities.

Number and type of lifts. How many chairlifts does the mountain have? How fast do they travel? How many skiers are they capable of transporting per hour? Some mountains have new chairlifts that are capable of carrying four or more skiers at a time at an impressively fast pace. Other mountains have slow means of transportation that often result in annoying long lift lines. A little advance research into this area may make the difference between having to wait in lift lines for forty-five minutes or fifteen minutes.

Are there lodges on the mountain? Many skiers like having the option of eating lunch, taking a break, or stopping for a drink on the mountain. Most modern ski resorts have two or more lodges on the mountain that include restaurants and a small ski shop. Generally the smaller mountains only have one "base lodge." If you ski with chil-

Modern ski resorts have hotel rooms that are comfortable and spacious.

dren, for instance, having a place to get off the mountain where they can warm up may be important to you.

Transportation. If your hotel is located beyond walking distance from the mountain, it's important to make sure there is some form of public transportation to transport you to the ski lifts. Often the hotel will have an hourly shuttle provided as a courtesy service. A few questions asked when you make your reservations will ensure that you don't end up "stranded."

Are ski schools and day care centers available? If this is your first ski experience or you're traveling with young children, you may want to ensure that the ski resort has a ski school or day care center that will meet your needs. For more on skiing with children, see Chapter 10.

Non-skiing activities. This becomes especially important if you are traveling with non-skiing companions. You may also find that not everyone in your party wishes to ski all day. One good source of information is the local tourist bureau for the destination you wish to visit. Another advantage to alternate activities is that they are a terrific way to meet new people. In fact, skiing in general is a tremendously social activity.

Do they make snow? Most ski resorts make snow. The question is how often do they make snow, and how thorough is their coverage? Manmade snow can make the difference between shredding the bottom of your skis or having an enjoyable "gouge free" skiing experience. Another consideration is *what percentage of the mountain's snow is manmade?* Manmade snow is "slower" than natural snow. Many skiers don't enjoy skiing on mountains where the coverage is primarily manmade. You may also want to look into whether or not they groom the manmade snow ... and how often.

Nightlife. Après ski activities are part of the fun of the skiing vacation. Some resorts offer little more après ski activities than watching the pond melt outside your hotel window! Others have a wide variety of options.

Cost. What will your skiing vacation cost? In addition to the obvious expense of food, lodging, and lift tickets, look into the cost of transportation and other forms of entertainment.

One of the best ways to stretch your dollar is to shop for "package deals" that include transportation, lodging, and lift tickets. Often the packages are cheaper than purchasing these items separately. Some packages also include rental equipment as an option. If you are a new skier, this type of situation may be great for you.

Is rental equipment available? If you are planning on renting ski equipment once you arrive at the resort, this is obviously an important issue. In addition to the question of whether or not rental equipment is available, you should also ask about the quantity of equipment on hand and its age. Most ski shops have the latest models available for rent. The thinking is that you should be able to "demo" any potential purchases before you buy. Generally, avoid shops that don't offer a wide selection of modern rental equipment.

If you are traveling with children, you should also look into whether or not the rental shop carries their specific sizes.

Keep in mind, however, that you may save money by renting your equipment locally, where you live, rather than renting at the resort. Often resort shops charge more since they are aware of the fact that you have no choice but to rent from them.

WHERE SHOULD YOU GO?

Picking a resort can be confusing since there is an almost endless variety to choose from. If you're on a budget, you may decide to limit your choices to areas you can drive to. On the other hand, some of the most exclusive (and expensive) places are ski resorts. Perhaps more than any other sport, ski areas offer the widest range of accommodations, facilities, and price range.

So where should you go? Rather than recommend specific mountains, what follows is a general overview of some of the more popular.

Jackson Hole, Wyoming

Jackson Hole offers skiers two main mountains in an Old West atmosphere. *Rendezvous Mountain*, which rises up 4,139 feet, is the highest vertical rise of any resort in America. *Apres Vous Mountain*, located nearby, has a vertical rise of 2,170 feet. Between the two mountains there is something to satisfy skiers of all levels.

One of the more popular hotels in Jackson Hole is the Alpenhof Lodge, which is located at the base of the mountain and is close to all lifts. The Alpenhof Lodge also offers vacationers a four star restaurant, bar and bistro, game room, ski lockers, Jacuzzi™ and sauna, and many other luxuries.

Less expensive accommodations can be found at the Western Hotel, which is located twelve miles from the ski resort.

Contacting hotels in the Jackson Hole area can be difficult during the off-season. To obtain information, the best procedure is to call or write to the Jackson Hole Central Reservations: P.O. Box 2618, 140 East Broadway, Jackson Hole, WY 83001. (800) 443-6931; Fax: (307) 733-1286.

Schweitzer Mountain Resort, Idaho

Located seventy-five miles southeast of Spokane, Washington, Schweitzer Mountain has a vertical rise of 2,400 feet, lodging for 600, one high speed quad chair, and five double chairs. Many skiers choose Schweitzer Mountain over the more popular Sun Valley to avoid high costs and crowds. For further information, call or write: Schweitzer Mountain Resort, P.O. Box 815, Sandpoint, ID 83864. (208) 263-9555 or (800) 831-8810.

Sun Valley, Idaho

Sun Valley is one of the most established resorts in western America. Long known as a playground to various celebrities, Sun Valley offers skiers a vertical drop of 3,400 feet, 64 runs, 16 chairs, and 253 acres of snow making.

One of the more popular places to stay is the Sun Valley

Lodge, which is located approximately two miles from the ski area. The lodge is entirely self-sufficient and offers five restaurants, a ski shop, an outdoor skating rink, and transportation to the mountain every fifteen minutes. Prices are in the $150 per night range, although considerably cheaper deals are available depending upon the time of year. For information about the lodge and other Sun Valley accommodations, call (800) 635-8261 or (208) 622-4111. Additional tourist information can be obtained by calling (208) 726-3423.

For up-to-the-minute information about snow conditions in Sun Valley, call (800) 635-4150.

Snowmass, Colorado

Snowmass opened to the public in 1967 and has maintained a reputation as one of the best family resorts in the world. With a vertical drop of 3,015 feet, 14 chairlifts, and a lift capacity of 20,535 skiers per hour, Snowmass offers skiers some of the widest runs in North America. The *Big Burn* is over a half mile wide and was created when Indians burned trees to try to discourage settlers from staying. One of the nice aspects of the mountain is that it has three distinct peaks, all of which can be skied from the same base.

For information about conditions at Snowmass, call (303) 925-1211. Numerous hotels and condominiums are located both on the slopes and in Snowmass Village at the mountain's base.

Aspen, Colorado

Aspen is located about a twenty-minute drive from Snowmass and has a reputation of being a harder mountain to ski. However, if steep, challenging mogul field runs are your cup of tea, then Aspen Mountain may be for you! Aspen offers skiers a vertical drop of 3,267 feet, a lift capacity of 10,775 skiers per hour, 210 acres covered by snowmaking machinery (which is 35% of the resort), 7 chairlifts, and 1 gondola. For up-to-the-minute information about Aspen, call (303) 925-1220.

One of the attractions of Aspen is the town. Numerous shops, restaurants, hotels, bars, and discos are located near the base of the mountain. Aspen isn't cheap, though, and getting a reservation may require quite a bit of advance notice.

Heavenly Valley, California

Located on the California/Nevada border, Heavenly Valley offers skiers a vertical drop of 2,900 feet (Nevada side) or 3,600 feet (California side) and covers over twenty square miles of terrain. Heavenly Valley, with a run of five and a half miles, has one of the longest ski runs in western America. One of the attractions for some vacationers at Heavenly Valley is the fact that there are gambling casinos and a wide variety of nightlife available in Nevada. For current information about Heavenly Valley, call (916) 541-1330. Numerous skiing/gambling/hotel packages are available.

Mammoth, California

Located about a six-hour drive north of Los Angeles, Mammoth Mountain is the most popular ski area in California. With a vertical drop of 3,100 feet, an elevation of 11,053 feet, over 150 runs, 30 lifts, 2 gondolas, and a lift capacity of 42,000 per hour, Mammoth is capable of serving an enormous volume of skiers during its peak season.

One of appealing aspects of Mammoth is the fact that the average winter temperature is about 35 degrees! If sunshine, fresh powder, and a seemingly unlimited variety of runs are your idea of a good time, then Mammoth may be for you. One possible drawback to Mammoth is the fact that weekends can get fairly crowded due to the ease of access from major cities such as Los Angeles. For up-to-the-minute information about conditions, hotels, and ski packages in Mammoth, call (619) 934-2571.

Killington, Vermont

Killington is one of the most popular mountains in northeast America. With a vertical drop of 3,173 feet, 15 chairlifts, a gondola, and a lift capacity of 30,827 skiers per hour, Killington is capable of handling a large volume of skiers. The one word that many skiers feel describes this mountain best is "variety." *Outer Limits* is known as one of the steepest, most moguled covered runs around ... and should please expert skiers. *Snowshed*, on the other hand, is ideally suited to the novice skier. For current information about Killington Ski Resort, call (802) 773-1500 or (802) 422-3333.

Park City, Utah

Park City is Utah's largest ski resort and is also known as one of the most "free spirited" resorts. Ironically it's also known as one of the most crowded. The Mountain features a vertical drop of 3,100 feet, 650 acres of open bowl skiing, 82 trails, 13 chairlifts, 1 gondola, and a lift capacity of 18,700 per hour. With nearly 50% of the mountain devoted to intermediate trails, Park City is a good choice for the pleasure skiers. Information can be obtained by calling (801) 649-8111.

Okemo, Vermont

Located in Ludlow, Vermont, Okemo is known as an ideal mountain for intermediate skiers. The mountain features 70 trails, a vertical drop of 2,150 feet, 8 chairlifts, 2 T-bars, and a longest run of 4 1/2 miles. The one drawback to the area is that there's not much to do except ski. Call (802) 228-4041 to get the latest information.

Vail, Colorado

Vail was one of the first modern ski resort complexes to achieve national recognition. The entire resort is extremely well planned, although in recent years it has begun to grow beyond its designer's original parameters. Overall, the entire resort is extremely convenient and the mountain's lift network services skiers well. Vail has a vertical drop of 3,200 feet, 3,784 acres of skiing terrain, 2,584 acres of bowl skiing on the backside, 320 acres of snow making, and a lift capacity of 35,020 skiers per hour. For current information, call (303) 476-5601.

Winter Park, Colorado

Winter Park is known as an intermediate/advanced mountain. Most of the trails are relatively narrow and bordered by high rows of trees. The mountain has a vertical drop of 2,220 feet, 106 trails, and a lift capacity of 28,210 skiers per hour. The resort is also less developed than some of Colorado's better known resorts. However, if you want to avoid the crowds, this giant mountain may be for you. Winter Park is also known for its strong children's ski program. Information about hotels, conditions, and ski packages can be received by calling (303) 726-5514.

Mont Ste.-Anne, Quebec, Canada

Mont Ste.-Anne is known as the nicest ski area in Quebec, Canada. Like many large mountains located near major cities, weekends at this resort can be crowded. The mountain features a vertical drop of 2,050 feet, a lift capacity of

17,157 skiers per hour, snow making on 85% of the terrain, 1 gondola, 7 chairlifts, 5 T-bars, and 1 pony lift. Information can be obtained by calling (514) 861-6679 or (418) 827-4561.

Lake Louise, Alberta, Canada

If powder skiing in big bowls is your idea of a good time, then this resort is for you! *Paradise Bowl* offers over 400 acres alone. The mountain has 43 designated runs, thousands of acres of skiable terrain and a longest run of 5 miles, 1 gondola, 6 chairs, 2 T-bars, a rope tow, and snow making on 75% of the mountain southface. With an average temperature of 14 degrees, plan on dressing warm! Information can be obtained by calling (403) 522-3555 or (403) 256-8473.

The nearby town of Banff offers vacationers numerous shops, restaurants, and some of the most beautiful winter scenery in western Canada.

Alta, Utah

With an average snowfall of 500 inches, Alta is frequented by "powder hounds." The mountain is most known for its powder bowls and open terrain. Some vacationers choose to stay in Salt Lake City, which is located twenty-six miles away, although there are hotels and condominiums located within walking distance to the lifts. Call (801) 742-3333 for current information.

Mt. Bachelor, Oregon

This mountain is consistently rated as one of the top ten resorts in America. A recent $20 million renovation and expansion project has given the area a face-lift. The mountain has a vertical drop of 3,100 feet, 11 chairlifts, 54 runs, and more high speed lift capacity than any area on the west coast. With an annual snowfall of sixteen feet, Mt. Bachelor offers skiers one the most consistent ski conditions in western America. One drawback is the fact that the area's average temperature is 16 degrees ... you will need a hat.

One of the more popular hotels is the Inn of the Seventh Mountain, which is rated as a triple A, four diamond resort and is the closest lodging to the mountain. Another option is to rent a condo or a house, which can be had for as low as $70 per night. The Holiday Motel offers rooms as cheap as $32 per night. For further information, call (503) 382-2442.

Breckenridge, Colorado

Breckenridge began as a mining settlement in 1860 and has continued to grow ever since. The resort is known as a first-class venue for world-class competition events. With 16 modern ski lifts, 1,526 acres of skiable terrain, and a vertical drop of 2,610 feet, Breckenridge is capable of handling a large volume of skiers efficiently. For up-to-the-minute information, call (303) 453-2368.

Copper Mountain, Colorado

Copper Mountain is one of Colorado's less crowded resorts. The reason is that the "resort" at the base of the mountain is basically nonexistent. However, if you are seeking crowdless skiing, romantically quiet nights, and an intimate atmosphere, then Copper Mountain may be for you. The mountain has a vertical drop of 1,200 feet and is made up of both huge, wide open areas and tree-lined trails. Overall, Copper Mountain is good for intermediate skiers seeking a variety of terrain. Information can be obtained by calling (800) 458-8386 or (303) 486-2277.

Whistler/Blackcomb, British Columbia, Canada

These two mountains, with vertical drops of 5,006 feet (Whistler) and 5,280 feet (Blackcomb), offer skiers the two largest vertical drops in North America. With a longest run of 7 miles, 214 major trails, seemingly countless bowls, and an annual snowfall of 450 inches, it's easy to see why the area is so popular. Unfortunately, this resort can also be extremely crowded during peak seasons. If you can visit the mountains in the off-season, however, you are in for a treat. Information can be obtained by calling (604) 932-3434 (Whistler), (604) 932-3141 (Blackcomb), or (800) 777-0185.

Squaw Valley, California

Located forty-two miles from the Reno, Nevada airport, Squaw Valley offers skiers 32 lifts, a 150 passenger cable car, a high speed gondola, lots of quad chairlifts, and an average of 450 inches of snow. Conditions at Squaw Valley are consistent enough to have attracted the Olympic Games in the past. The mountain has a vertical drop of 2,850 feet, 8,300 skiable acres, and a breathtaking view of Lake Tahoe. As with all the resorts located on the California/Nevada Border, vacationers have the option of visiting the casinos and nightlife in Nevada. Information can be obtained by calling (800) 545-4530 or (916) 583-6985.

Beaver Creek, Colorado

This smaller resort appeals to vacationers wishing to get away from the peak season crowds often present at nearby Vail. In fact, Vail is only a short shuttle ride away, giving vacationers the option of skiing either mountain. Beaver Creek has a vertical drop of 3,800 feet and 21 miles of skiable terrain of which 50% is designated as intermediate. Information can be had by calling (303) 925-5300.

Jay Peak, Vermont

Jay Peak opened its slopes in 1957 and has grown slowly but consistently ever since. The mountain receives a lot of Canadian visitors, who find the convenience of the short drive across the border appealing. In fact, Montreal is only one and a half hours away. With a vertical drop of 2,000 feet, 28 trails, and a lift capacity of just under 4,000 skiers per hour, Jay Peak isn't one of the larger resorts in Vermont, but it usually is one of the least crowded. Information can be obtained by calling (802) 626-3305.

10

Children and Skiing

Children can learn to ski as early as three years old! In fact, they quickly turn into little bundled-up snowplowing tanks that seem to have the ability to tackle any slope you put them on. They have more flexibility than most adults and generally view skiing as something fun rather than a feared challenge to be overcome.

Actually, a child's view of skiing is often simpler and purer than an adult's. Watch an average four-year-old plowing down a hill—he's not concerned with his stance or how parallel his skis are. He's simply skiing and letting his body respond to the terrain as it's encountered. If he suddenly gets tossed to the left, he goes with it, and generally recovers. His view of the whole matter is simple and fun. In fact, if you want to improve your own skiing ability, try to view skiing with the same exuberance as a child! Let go of what you think you should look like and simply ski.

FEAR

An often heard statement relating to children and skiing is: "Lack of fear is one of the things kids have over adults when it comes to skiing, which allows them to learn faster than adults." Well, most kids that is. Actually, contrary to what most books claim, children *can be terrified* of the idea of skiing at first. For example, two four-year-old brothers recently learned to ski during a week-long trip to Vermont. The first brother put on his skis and from day one bombed down any slope he was put on. If he fell, he laughed hysterically. His brother, on the other hand, spent his time sitting in the snow and crying, apparently hating the whole concept of skiing.

How much exposure children have to snow prior to their first skiing experience may indicate how scared they will be. A youngster who lives in Vermont and is exposed to winter snow from birth will probably not be scared when skis are put on him for the first time. Conversely, a four-year-old from Florida, who has never seen snow or skis before, may be terrified of the slippery, cold, wet snow that he can't walk on.

Another statement often heard relating to kids and skiing is: "A child doesn't get hurt as easily as an adult when he falls, which is another reason kids aren't as scared." While there's a lot of truth in this statement due to the fact that most kids "go with" a fall rather than fight it, don't fool yourself. If a child falls hard on hard pack or ice, he's going to hurt!

Keeping the above statements in mind, however, it is true that children are generally less fearful of skiing once they get past the initial acclimation period. As an adult, you know the consequences of a broken leg, and so you may enter into your ski training with a certain amount of apprehension. We saw one middle-aged woman who was so nervous about hurting herself that when she fell over while standing still, the tension in her body prevented her from "going with the fall" ... and she broke her leg! Obviously, learning to ski with that kind of worry and concern is practically impossible. Children, for the most part, aren't concerned or aware of the possibility of injury.

A young skier finds it easier to simply "grab" the poma lift and hang on!

EQUIPMENT

Your child will need the same equipment as an adult skier does. Fortunately—since you'll be "renewing" your child's clothing and equipment every two years or so—ski clothing and equipment for kids do not cost as much as adult gear; although you can easily spend over $200 for skis, about $150 or more for bindings, and $250 for boots for an average ten-year-old.

Equipment for tots, of course, doesn't cost as much. Name-brand skis for your toddler can set you back over $100. K2's "Ninja" skis, for example, cost $150 and feature Ninja Turtle graphics. Bindings for your toddler's skis can be had for under $100. Tyrolia's 520 is a popular model and is priced at $75.

Toddler boots range in price from about $75 to over $100. Although a lot of ski equipment and clothing gets "handed down" to younger children, you may always want to invest in new boots. Secondhand boots may not offer adequate protection and support for your child's feet, or even worse, may be too small. Considering how tight a ski boot can be when it is fastened, it's best to avoid the possibility of damaging your child's foot by always investing in new boots.

When shopping for ski boots for younger children, take out the boot's inner lining and check to see if it fits your child's foot. One of the quickest ways to check initially to see if a boot is too big or small is to remove the lining and hold it against the child's foot.

Unlike adult boots, it's acceptable to purchase children's ski boots that are *slightly* oversized to accommodate expected growth. How oversized? Generally, a quarter inch of play in the heel is acceptable; more than that and the boot is probably too big. If you buy a slightly oversized boot, you can use wedges to take up the extra heel space. As your child grows during the season you can remove the wedges or shave them down.

Another important consideration when buying boots is warmth. Nothing will turn a child off skiing quicker than cold feet! Look for boots that fit, or that are slightly oversized while your child is wearing *two pairs* of socks. Also check to see if she can wiggle her toes with the boot buckled. If she can't, the boot is probably too small and won't provide enough warmth. Keep in mind that *fit* and *comfort* are the primary objectives.

Fortunately, there is a wide selection of equipment to choose from, so you should be able to find equipment to meet your child's needs regardless of age, skiing ability, or size. Most of the major ski equipment companies make boots and skis for both juniors and tots, often with numerous models for each age group. If you are unfamiliar with ski equipment, check in some ski magazines to find out what the brand names are. *Ski Magazine*, for example, is an excellent source of up-to-date reports on what equipment is "hot" and what's not. Another good source of information is a ski school, especially if your child is already enrolled in some type of program.

A note on bindings, however: look for ones that are *easy to operate*. Marker, Geze, Solomon, and Tyrolia, for example, all make junior bindings that operate simply enough to enable a young child to manipulate them with gloves on.

You may want to set your child's binding a bit looser than you would your own. Children tend to fall more often than adults, partly because they take more jumps and aren't as cautious as we full-grown skiers. By setting their bindings a little on the loose side, you'll ensure that they will release when they take that back gainer with a half twist off the mogul.

One way to stretch the life of your child's ski equipment is to purchase it as close to the ski season as possible. Considering how fast some youngsters grow, this may increase the "usable" life of the clothing and boots (sizewise).

Another way to save money is allow everyday winter clothes to do double duty as ski clothes (assuming you live where it snows). Gloves, mittens, hats, parkas, and snow suits that are worn to school can also be used on the slopes.

SKI SCHOOLS

Ski schools can be roughly broken down into two categories: *day care centers* that also offer ski lessons, and *ski schools* that only teach skiing.

Most ski resorts do offer extensive child care programs that not only involve ski classes, but also usually offer some type of after-ski activities as well. You can drop your children off in the morning, enjoy a full day skiing with your spouse or friend, and then retrieve them in the afternoon. If your child is young and you plan to use the day care/ski school on a daily basis, you may want to call ahead to see what the resort offers. The three main considerations are:

Ski school also gives children the chance to make new friends.

1. *Does the day care program offer numerous activities other than skiing?* The average three-year-old doesn't want to ski all day ... or even all morning for that matter. What other activities does the day care center offer?

2. *Are ski lessons available throughout the day?* Some day care/ski schools only offer ski lessons for a limited amount of time during some part of the day. Ideally, your child should be able to participate in skiing activities whenever he wants. Many day care/ski schools offer lessons anytime the child wishes. Usually there's an added charge for the additional ski lessons.

3. *Where is the day care located?* Naturally, a day care/ski school needs to be conveniently located. While this seems obvious, there are a few surprises waiting unwary vacationers out there. One California day care center, which also advertises ski lessons, is located two miles from the mountain! An obvious inconvenience.

One thought to keep in mind, however, before enrolling your child in a ski school/day care program is the fact that a ski school is a *school*. If your child hasn't been exposed to some sort of school, day care, or other environment that involves socializing with other children, it may be best not to enroll him in a ski school, but to teach him yourself.

Ski School

A *ski school* differs from a day care/ski school in that a ski school's primary function is to teach skiing, while a day care center basically baby-sits ... and also offers ski lessons. Some things to consider when selecting a ski school for your junior skier are:

Does it teach a system? Ask one of the instructors or the school director what program or system they use. Ideally, the school should have an integrated progressive program with well-defined goals and skills at each level of the system. If they don't, you can't be assured that your child will be put in a class that fits his needs and is aimed at his specific skill level. Naturally, you want to avoid having your child put in a class that is either too slow or too advanced for him. For example, avoid schools that group all the students into one "morning class" or one "afternoon class."

You also want to know that as your child's skill improves, he's not going to outgrow the school. A ski school shouldn't just teach basics; it should have the ability to teach your child advanced skills when he is ready.

In addition to being able to explain what system the school teaches and how it's integrated into each age group, ask the instructor what his philosophy of teaching is. Listen for words like *fun* and *enjoyable* as well as terms such as *progressive* and *integrated*. Avoid overly gung-ho instructors who want to get your child racing and competing as soon as possible. All ski instructors should understand that the primary purpose of skiing is *fun!* While this may seem obvious to most people, keep in mind that there are some instructors out there whose primary concern is cultivating future world-class racers.

Are children's classes taught separately from the adult program? Avoid ski schools that want to put your children in the adult classes. Participating in an adult class won't be fun for your child and may cause resentment from the adult participants who may not like having to take a class with "kids." Some parents are guilty of doing this in the interest of keeping their children with them. If you want to ski with your children or want the family to ski together, do it after class.

What is the school scheduling like? Ideally, you should be able to put your youngster in a class pretty much any time of day. For example, if you want to have your child enrolled in ski school every day of a week-long vacation, you may want to call ahead to ensure their scheduling will permit it. Conversely, you may not want your child in an "all day" program if you want to ski with him a portion of the day. A few phone calls before you put your money down will help ensure that you pick a resort with a ski school that will fit your specific needs.

TEACHING YOUNG CHILDREN

Odds are you will be your child's first instructor if he or she is less than three years old. Teaching kids in this age group can be fairly simple since you can teach with "hands on" contact. Keep in mind that children six years old and less tend to ski in a "sitting" position. Rather than try to correct their posture, let them ski in the position they find naturally. Children in this age group are rapidly developing coordination and balance and will often learn faster if left to their own devices. Also, just because you are dealing with young children doesn't mean you have to limit their skiing activities to the "bunny hills." In fact, this age group will often be ready for more advanced conditions sooner than older students!

No Poles

Children six years old and younger will learn faster if they are not burdened with ski poles for the first few lessons. Initially, the children will be learning new coordination involving balance, weight distribution, direction control, and independent leg movement, all of which are complicated by also having to hang onto ski poles. Also, you eliminate the possibility of some youngster discovering he has acquired an excellent new jousting rod!

So, how do you teach young kids to ski? Some methods you can use are:

Ski with the child between your legs. The advantage here is that the child immediately gets to enjoy the sensation of skiing while you control direction and speed. Also, the child begins to learn what turning feels like, which can be a quicker way of learning than trying to "explain" the mechanics of a snowplow turn to a four-year-old.

One possible disadvantage to this method is that the child may become overly dependent on the adult. It can create the "carry me" syndrome on skis.

Another disadvantage for the adult is that skiing with a child between your legs is a thigh burner if the child is small!

Hold her skis. You'll have to ski backwards to do this. What you do is bend forward and hold the tips of her skis to control her direction and speed. This lets the child "feel" what the turn should be like, which can be the quickest way to learn. This method really only works with small children.

Holding the tips of the child's skis works well with kids who are scared of falling or losing control. Your presence and reassurance can go a long way towards alleviating their fears.

Be aware, however, that skiing backwards and bent over while holding the child's skis can be hard on your back.

Use your poles. Hold your pole out to the side (pointed end towards you) and have the child hold the other end. This is an excellent way to control a child's speed and keep him close to you. Without some form of contact with the instructor, some children may "downhill it" from the word go.

Another variation is to use a long pole (such as a slalom gate pole) and ski down the hill with two or three students on each side of you. This can be an excellent way to control a small group of students.

TEACHING CONCEPTS FOR ALL AGES

The methods mentioned above are not that effective with older children. Some concepts to keep in mind when teaching children of any age are:

Talk simply. Adults tend to over-complicate simple instructions. For example, rather than try to describe accurately how a snowplow can slow a skier down, simply show them what a snowplow looks like.

Adapt to their psychology. Children don't want to go to school ... they want to have fun. Rather than "conduct a lesson" on how to ski, organize a "play session" that just happens to be done on skis. The minute children start to feel they're in school, they lose interest.

Start on flat ground. This seems exceedingly obvious but it's surprising how hard it can be to find truly "flat" ground in a ski area. Besides making the initial learning process easier, teaching on the flats will assist you in keeping track of the children if you are teaching more than one.

Let them ski. If a child wants to point his skis downhill and simply "go," let him. Obviously, you shouldn't teach on a dangerously steep or crowded slope. Speed is what makes skiing fun for most kids. Rather than inhibit their enthusiasm, let them experience the joy and exhilaration under your control and guidance.

Teach them to stop. Conversely to the above statement, knowing how to stop gives skiers of all levels confidence. Teaching your children how to stop early on also has the advantage of ensuring (somewhat) that they won't injure themselves by skiing into something. Teaching them how to stop can be as simple as showing them how to "sit down" and fall if they feel out of control.

Keep them moving. Children are impatient and can have lots of energy. Nothing can cause a child to lose concentration faster than having to stand around for long periods of time. The mere act of moving on skis will give the children's attention something to focus on.

Keep in mind that the main objective is to ski! By keeping everybody moving you will be assured that you're not boring your class by talking too much. Movement also prevents the kids from getting cold! Obviously, you want to avoid having your students get chilled.

Tell them when they do well. Children need, like, and enjoy approval from adults. Reward work well done with compliments. If you have a group, you can even give out daily prizes for the "best snowplow of the day," or "fastest skier of the morning." Conversely, don't "play favorites." If one child's skiing ability begins to far exceed that of the others, don't turn her into a teacher's pet.

Pay attention to each child. Often the child who is doing the worst may be the one who is in need of the most attention. For instance, a child may have an irrational fear of falling due to a lack of information. Explaining to the child that falling in the soft snow won't hurt and can even be fun may improve her skiing ability. Ignoring the child, however, because she's not learning fast enough won't solve anything and may damage the child's confidence permanently.

Teach them one thing at a time. Trying to cram too much information at once can often lead to a student not retaining any of it. For example, it's better for a child to learn how to snowplow well than to "sort of understand" a bunch of concepts but be unable to perform any of them. It's better to be repetitive on one or two skills than to show twenty skills one time each.

The more skiing the better. Remember, the whole point of the day is to learn to ski! The sooner you get them moving, the better ... and the more fun! Also, kids hate to stop.

While an adult might want to take a breather to admire the view ... a child sees the stop as an interruption to fun. Don't worry about overtaxing four-year-olds. Generally, they'll let you know when they want to stop ... at which point they will march into the lodge for some hot chocolate and a hamburger, rest a while, and then hit the slopes for another nonstop session.

Make it fun. The bottom line is if the kids aren't having fun, they won't learn anything and you probably won't have a good day either. For example, if a child falls down, applaud the fall and fall down yourself—and then instruct the whole class to fall over. Tactics such as this will not only keep the day fun but will also help alleviate irrational fears.

Teach safety rules. The fact that some youngsters are so "fear free" makes it important to teach them basic rules relating to ski safety early on. Simple concepts such as always looking at what is in front of you and don't ski into anyone or anything should be taught early on.

GAMES

One of the best ways to teach children is to play games that not only help them develop new skills but also add to the "fun" of the experience. Following are some games you can play.

Do as I do! As stated above, it's easier to "show" children how to do something than to explain it. Games like "Simon Says" can be an excellent way to run children through various skiing body positions. This method can be a lot more effective than running kids through a series of "un-fun" drills.

Follow the leader. "Follow the leader" combined with "Do as I do" is an excellent way to teach direction control. You can teach kids to snowplow by telling them to copy your body position and then lead them through a series of slow "S" turns as you play follow the leader. Remember to ski on a variety of terrain so your students are exposed to different types of skiing environments. Also, skiing on different kinds of slopes helps keep the experience fun for the children.

Tag, you're it!. A game of tag is an excellent way to get kids to practice direction control, speed control, and stopping. Play the game just as you would without skis. Someone is appointed as being "it" until he tags another child, who then becomes "it."

Kid slalom. This another good game to practice turning and direction control. Place the kids in your class at ten to fifteen foot intervals down the hill. Have the uppermost child ski the course; when he reaches the bottom he then stops and becomes the bottommost "pole." At this point, the new uppermost child skis "the course."

Slalom. If you're not teaching a large group, you can lay out a slalom course with ski poles, articles of clothing (such as gloves), or natural objects (such as bumps in the snow). As with the above game, skiing a slalom course teaches direction and speed control.

Play catch. Developing independent upper and lower body coordination is an important step towards becoming a good skier. Skiing down a hill while playing catch with a ball or glove forces independent coordination and is a lot of fun! You can have your class ski in a line while they toss an object from one end to the other or they can ski down in pairs while playing catch.

One thing to keep in mind is to make sure your students are aware that they have to watch where they are going rather than becoming totally obsessed with the game. With young children it may be best to pick a slope that is "obstacle free."

Contests. Games such as "who can make the most turns between these two poles" are both fun and invaluable learning tools. Other contests can be as simple as "who can ski the fastest." Be imaginative.

Fetch. You can use this game while teaching the kids direction control. It's also useful when learning how to walk uphill. For example, challenge the class "who can get my glove first" and then throw it a few feet uphill. The winner can be rewarded with an aprés ski treat.

Holding hands. Holding hands is another game that helps develop independent upper and lower body coordination. As with playing catch, this game can be played with the entire class holding hands or with the group skiing in pairs.

A variation on holding hands is to have each pair hold hands while facing each other and standing side by side. As they ski down the hill, the child facing downhill skis around his partner (who is skiing backwards) and pulls him around until they reverse positions (the child who was previously skiing forward is now skiing backwards). The idea is for the pair to keep skiing in circles around each other as they travel down the slope.

11

Mental Aspects

Although skiing is an extremely physical sport, it is also very much a "head" game as well. In fact, most skiers experience a conflict between their body and mind from day one! The problem is that your brain thinks it has sense enough to see that sliding down a hill at high speed is actually an excellent way to get hurt! What skiing requires of you physically is often in direct conflict with what *seems* to make sense. For example, when novice skiers feel out of control they instinctively want to "sit back" on their skis ... which throws their weight back and usually results in a fall. The mind incorrectly assumes that sitting back away from the hill is the sensible choice.

To ski well you will have to learn to control what's going on in your conscious mind as you ski.

RELAXATION

Put your hand on a table (or anywhere you can relax it completely). Now as fast as you can, pull your hand to your chest.

Now try the same exercise again ... but this time tense all the muscles in your hand, arm, and shoulder before you attempt to pull your hand to your chest as fast as you can. Ideally, have a friend signal you to move each time by clapping.

As you can see, your reaction time is much faster when you are relaxed. When your muscles are tense, you have to relax them first before you can react — which slows you down.

This same concept applies to skiing. Imagine you are skiing along and suddenly and unexpectedly hit a series of bumps. If your legs are tight and unforgivable, you will most likely fall since you won't react in time. Conversely, if your legs are relaxed, you'll be able to "absorb" the bumps by bending your knees as you go over them.

So how do you relax while standing on the edge of what your brain is telling you is a dangerously steep and slippery cliff? Well, first you must:

Get Focused

One way to control your mind is to keep it busy with something constructive relating to the activity you're doing. For example, as you connect your parallel turns, think, or even say out loud, "up" (as you unweight), and "down" (as you make the turn). Try to establish a rhythm—"up" ... "down" ... "up" ... "down."

This exercise accomplishes three things. First, it will give your mind something to focus on to "get it out of the way." Second, it will help your skiing by ensuring that you do stand up to unweight ... and then get back down as you turn. Third, it will establish a rhythm in your turns, which is important.

Plan Your Line

Another way to stay focused is to *plan your line*. Before you take a run, look ahead and pick out your course. As you ski the run, continue to look ahead and plan where you will make the next three to five turns. The idea is two-fold. First, planning the course will keep your mind busy so it can't interfere with your skiing. Second, *planning your line is important* because it enables you to see tricky areas, icy spots, and other hazards before you hit them.

Visualize Your Run

In unison with planning your line, you should also *visualize your run*. Give yourself a clear picture of what you should look like skiing the run and then let your body do it while your mind is busy analyzing the course.

Follow Another Skier

One of the best ways to turn your brain "off" is to *follow another skier*. Pick someone who is a better skier than you and simply follow her line. Without having to "think" about where you are going, your mind simply shuts off and goes along for the ride. Try this—you'll probably be amazed at how well you will ski.

Another reason skiing behind a better skier often makes you ski better is that your body, free of interference from your brain, "imitates" the form of the skier in front of you.

Another advantage to following an advanced skier is that you will experience (and learn from) the line she takes down the hill.

LETTING IT HAPPEN

"Just relax," said Richard to a concerned-looking Chipper. "You're a good skier—stop worrying about it and go!"

Suddenly, Chipper pushed off the lip with careless abandon and began a high speed descent through waist-deep powder—and skied it perfectly. When he reached the bottom, he looked amazingly calm, considering how worried he had been at lunch about skiing deep powder.

"How did you get over your anxiety about that run?" I later asked him while we were riding the chairlift.

Chipper explained to me that when Richard told him to relax, he did just that. "I simply let go and went for it," he explained. "Once I began my run I just let it happen ... I didn't really care about the outcome."

In other words, he turned his mind off—relaxed—and simply skied. Sometimes all that's needed to ski well is to *stop* thinking, and then simply "let it happen."

One way to keep your head clear is to keep skiing fun!

RUTS

At some point in your skiing career you are going to have a day when everything seems to be going wrong. No matter how hard you try, you just can't get into the flow of things. Your tips keep crossing, your edges want to catch (except not when you're turning), and your poles feel more like vaulting sticks than ski equipment. So how do you break out of a rut? Well, here are some ways that have worked for us:

Take a Break

Sometimes all that's needed to put some freshness into your skiing is to take a break! It may be that all you need is an hour in the lodge, or perhaps you should consider taking a day or more off. You can only attempt to "beat" yourself into submission by ordering your body around on the ski slopes for so long; eventually, it gets fed up with all the mental orders about how it should ski and "quits." Taking a break gives you time to unwind from all the self-induced stress so you can return to the slopes "fresh."

Taking a break often results in better skiing when you return to the slopes because your body is free to resolve the problem/problems you were having before. Without interference from your brain, your body can adjust "naturally" since you are now relaxed enough to allow it. For example, after a ski lesson your mind may be full of thoughts and commands from your instructor. Frustration begins to set in after the lesson as you "command" yourself to perform the skills taught during the class. With all this "mental" interference, most skiers find it impossible to perform well. Ironically, your body most likely has "retained" the new skill learned, but is unable to execute it because your head is too busy trying to "force" the issue. Taking a break at this point may help "turn off" your thoughts so you can then return to the slopes fresh and let yourself ski!

Ski Something Different

Another way to take a break is to ski a *different type of run or conditions*. It's a way of "taking a break" without taking your skis off! For example, if you have spent the morning trying to ski moguls but are having a bad time of it, changing location and going to ski flat powder for a while will take your mind off moguls. It may also return your confidence that took a beating in the mogul field. When you return to skiing moguls later in the day, or even a day or two later, you will probably find yourself skiing a lot better.

Locate the Problem

Before you can fix a problem, you need to identify it. For example, most skiers have a strong side and a weak side. They may find that it's easier to make a left turn than a right turn. So what's wrong with their weak side? They probably don't know because they've never really thought about it; they just know that they don't turn well in that direction. If you find yourself in this predicament, rather than ignore the problem like many skiers do, why not seek assistance in identifying what's wrong ... and then correcting it. One way to do this is to take a lesson. A qualified ski instructor will be able to explain to you exactly what you're doing wrong ... and then show you the correct solution.

In some instances you may be able to identify what's troubling your skiing on your own. For example, if you find that you always "slide" too far downhill when you do a "hockey stop," think about why that is. You'll most likely realize that you are not edging your skis enough to stop.

DEALING WITH FEAR

"I can't ... I'm scared!" said Suzanne Lacroix. She was about to ski her first black diamond run with her son Michel and his wife, Sylvie. She was scared because she was being "pushed" to ski a run that was beyond her ability.

Like Suzanne, most skiers occasionally experience some amount of fear while skiing. Actually, fear is often a good thing since it may prevent you from hurting yourself. In the same way it makes sense to be scared to jump off a high building, it also makes sense to fear skiing down a steep, icy, mogul-covered run if your skill level isn't up to the challenge. Fear only becomes a problem when it "paralyzes" your performance, which often happens when skiers exceed their comfort level.

Comfort Level

One way to deal with fear is to ski within your *comfort level*, which means to ski within the boundaries of your ability. By staying within your comfort level, you will not put yourself in a situation where you could possibly get hurt ... such as skiing on a hill that is too steep for your skill level. You can (and should) expand your comfort level by *gradually* exposing yourself to new challenges and/or by taking lessons to increase your skill in the areas you feel are weak.

Another important step in dealing with fear is to identify what is frightening you. For example, you may come to realize that you are experiencing fear because the people you are skiing with ski too fast for your comfort level. The hill isn't frightening you—the speed is. The solution would be simply to slow down until you're skiing at a speed that is comfortable. This may sound overly simple, but many skiers don't take the time to isolate what's scaring them. The result is they take a fall, and possibly get hurt, because they are too tense (from fear) to ski well.

Something you should keep in mind is that skiing *is* a high risk activity. In fact, for some skiers, that's part of its attraction. The adrenaline "rush" that comes with skiing, especially during your first few runs as a novice, is exciting *because* you feel it's a little dangerous. Just don't convince yourself you can't ski every time you feel a little fear. Learn to differentiate the real risks from natural nervousness.

12

Schools, Clubs, and Instructors

Learning to ski can be a lot of fun; it can also lead to a lot of frustration if you don't learn correctly from the start. The best way to learn, especially in the beginning, is with a qualified ski instructor who teaches through one of the excellent ski schools available at most resorts. By learning in this manner, you will excel at a faster rate than if you simply try to "wing it."

Another advantage to learning with an instructor is that you will be less likely to hurt yourself (or someone else) since you'll be taught strong basics such as stopping right from the start!

Perhaps one of the best reasons to enroll in ski school is the fact that *ski school students don't have to wait in lift lines!* Students and instructors use a "private" line that takes them straight to the front! If getting as much ski time in as possible is one of your priorities, then ski school may be for you.

PRIVATE OR GROUP LESSONS

One of the first decisions you will have to make is whether to take private or group lessons. *Private lessons* allow you to receive 100% of the teacher's attention. The lesson can also be devoted entirely to your specific skill level and needs. The one disadvantage to private instruction is that it can get extremely costly at some resorts. Incidentally, you most likely don't need private instruction during your first few hours on the slopes since the basic skills are fairly easy and don't really require intensive student-teacher interaction. Once you have mastered the basics, however, you may want to take a few private lessons.

Group lessons give you the opportunity to learn from

other people's mistakes; and they are considerably cheaper than private instruction. Another "plus" to group lessons is that you will meet a lot of other skiers whose skills are about the same as yours. If you are looking for skiing companions, a group lesson is a good place to meet them. On a recent ski trip, a friend of ours brought along his girlfriend who had never skied before. Each morning she took a group lesson and then would meet us for lunch so we could all ski together in the afternoon. It constantly amazed us how popular she had become on the slopes ... everywhere we went somebody knew her! All her new-found friends had been in ski class!

SELECTING THE SKI SCHOOL OR CLUB

What should you look for when selecting a ski school, a club, or an instructor? Well, you might want to consider:

Location. Where is the school located in relation to the ski area? One club in Canada, for instance, meets at different restaurants each week and then drives to the mountain. If you are traveling to a big resort, such as Vail, then the locations of the ski schools shouldn't be a problem since they're almost always located at the base of the mountain. If, however, you plan to ski at a small local mountain, then you may want to look into where the ski school meets.

Ski club or ski school. A ski school teaches skiing ... and generally doesn't do much else. A ski club, on the other hand, usually offers lessons in addition to numerous other activities such as dances, races, carnivals, and picnics. Ski clubs also often have preseason get-in-shape activities.

Children who live near a ski area may benefit from joining a ski club. In addition to getting a ride to the ski area with other club members, children benefit from the social interaction and the security of skiing with an instructor the majority of the time. If you live near a ski area, check into the local ski club!

If you are going on vacation, you most likely won't have much choice as to the ski school, especially once you have arrived, since most resorts only have one ski school at the base of the mountain that caters to vacationing skiers. However, if you have specific requirements, you may want to look into the mountain's ski school before you make your reservations.

Do they teach a system? Most established ski schools have some type of program designed to help the student progress rapidly. Although it's not as popular as it once was, the G.L.M. (Graduating Length Method) school of thought, for instance, was once used at almost all ski resorts. The G.L.M. school starts skiers out on extremely short skis so they can learn the basics quickly. The students then "graduate" to progressively longer skis as their skill increases. Students generally learn faster with this method since they don't have to contend with 195cm skis from day one.

Today, most resorts use the *American Teaching System*, which teaches students clean, simple, fundamental techniques right from the beginning.

There are other methods taught too. The point to keep in mind is that the ski school should *have a method*.

Get classified in advance. Get your skiing ability evaluated before you go to sign up for the class. This way you will know in advance what type of class you should be in. Most ski schools use a combination of "on the slopes" evaluation, a written test, and discussion between the student and instructor. You want to avoid ending up in a class that's either too advanced or too simple for your specific skill level.

Is the instructor associated with the ski school? Although there are some excellent independent instructors out there, it's generally a good idea to deal only with instructors who are working for the resort's ski school. By doing so, you help eliminate the risk of getting burned financially; you are also assured that you're getting quality instruction since most ski schools have strict standards for their instructors.

Is the instructor certified? One way to practically insure that you will get a good lesson is to ask for a *fully certified instructor*.

Do you like the instructor? Learning to ski should be fun. And if you don't like your instructor, you are probably not going to enjoy the lesson. If you feel uncomfortable with the instructor assigned to you, ask for someone else. At a large resort there are usually dozens of instructors on staff, so you should be able to find someone right for you.

13

Competition

If you enjoy participating in competitive sports, then skiing probably has something to offer you! From the local Nastar race course to the Olympics, skiing offers competitive opportunities for skiers of all levels.

NASTAR

Almost every mountain in the United States has a Nastar Race Course. Nastar, introduced by *Ski Magazine* in 1968, stands for the National Standard Ski Race. Nastar awards skiers a handicap rating so skiers from different mountains and courses, skiing on different days, can compare times. The concept is to make ski racing available to all skiers. If you are interested in getting into racing, getting involved with Nastar is an excellent way to start!

SLALOM

Probably the most popular event in competitive skiing is the *slalom*. Slalom is a game of speed as racers ski around a series of "gates" against the clock and each other. Races are won and lost by *hundredths* of a second, and style isn't as important as time and speed. Some concepts to keep in mind when skiing slalom are:

Ski the shortest path. Slalom skiers are often seen skating, or taking a step as they come around a gate. The idea is to ski the shortest line possible between gates; the "step" puts them on a shorter course by eliminating wide sweeping turns.

Get a good start. Many racers feel they can win a race with a good start. Although there is an endless variety of techniques, the most common is to plant your poles in front of your body while sitting back (think of yourself as a "coiled spring") and at the end of the countdown explode out of the gate by "launching" yourself.

Lean into the finish. Considering that races are won by hundredths of a second, you want to trip the clock as soon as you reach the finish line. Since your skis are so close to the ground the finish line won't "see" them. As you approach the finish line lean in front of your skis with your hand to trip the finish light and stop the clock.

Ski through the finish. Some racers relax during the last few moments of a race when they feel they are past the hard part. Once again, *speed is everything* in slalom; you don't want to "quit" until you are through the finish. One trick is to imagine that the finish line is actually beyond where the real finish is. By aiming for the imaginary finish, you will ski full power through the real finish.

Memorize the course. Study the course before you ski it. You don't want to wait to discover an obstacle until you are skiing on top of it. Many racers find that *visualizing their race* helps to prepare them mentally.

The best way to get to know the course is to walk it. That way you can get an up-close look at the gates so you can plot how you will ski them.

Don't overdo it. Although speed is the name of the game, you don't want to ski so fast that you lose control and fall. An average race that you finish is better than a wildly fast and out of control race that ends in a fall—on the wrong side of the finish line!

Use anything that works. One of the fun things about slalom is that *anything goes!* For example, you may find that a quick snowplow check before your turn around the gate may be the quickest way to slow down. Or you may find that putting your weight on your uphill ski will help you ski in a faster line. The point is, use whatever will help you ski the fastest course!

GIANT SLALOM

Giant slalom, as its name implies, is basically a long slalom course. One plus (depending on circumstances) on a giant slalom course is that you may get a chance to make up for a mistake that slowed you down since the course is long enough for you to "catch up." All the concepts talked about above apply to giant slalom. Keep in mind, however, that on a longer course simply "surviving" the duration comes into play. On a shorter slalom course you can give all you have from the start. On a giant slalom course you may have to pace yourself somewhat.

DOWNHILL

Downhill is simple—you point your skis downhill and go. Well, it's simple unless you fall! Downhill racing takes tremendous strength and ability to avoid injury. If you hit an unexpected mogul at high speed (say over sixty miles an hour) and are thrown, you most likely won't enjoy the results. With downhill, it is critical you plan your race.

The key to going as fast as possible is to keep your skis flat. Even when you turn you want to use as little of the ski's edge as possible since edging your skis slows them down.

14

The History of Skiing

One of the amazing things about modern recreational downhill skiing is how *new* a sport it is. Skiers of just a few decades ago never dreamed of the control we now have over our skis—or the speeds that even novice skiers now obtain. Until the many innovations in equipment (most of which took place in the last sixty years or so), downhill skiing really wasn't safe.

However, while downhill skiing is a relatively new sport, skiing as a means of *transportation* has been used by man for thousands of years. In fact, on the island of Rodoy, Norway, scientists have found stone etchings depicting a man on skis that are thought to be at least 4,000 years old! And further evidence that early man used skis as a means of winter transportation can be determined by dating skis found in the bogs of Norway, Finland, and Sweden. One such ski found in Sweden is believed to date back to 2000 B.C.

EARLY SKIERS

The first skiers may have used animal bones as a type of snowshoe. Actually, most ancient skis that have been recovered are as much snowshoe as ski and were used primarily as a means of transportation along flat ground.

Our ancestors used strips of animal skin, plant vines, and leather thongs to tie their feet to their skis. These early bindings were loose, making any type of controlled turn while in motion impossible. Without the ability to stop or turn, speed was also out of the question. Due to these "equipment" limitations, early skiers were limited to a "snowshoe-like" forward shuffle.

Few cultures are as closely tied to skiing as the Norwegians. In fact, the word "ski" is the Norwegian word for a type of snowshoe once used in the Old World.

If you had been a Norwegian Viking living around 1000 A.D., you might have worshiped the god (Ull) and goddess (Skade) of skiing. Both are mentioned in written accounts of the period.

One of the most well-known historical moments in Norwegian skiing history took place during the Norwegian Civil War of 1206 when the king of Norway sent two solders to carry his son over the snow-covered mountains. The solders, known as "birchlegs" because they wrapped their legs with birch to protect themselves from the freezing temperatures, carried the infant across the mountains on skis. The event is commemorated each year in Norway at the Birkebeinerrennet Cross-country Race, which traces the birchlegs' thirty-five-mile crossing and attracts thousands of participants. If you are interested in cross-country skiing, you may want to look into attending this event.

Skiing is also deeply rooted in Sweden's history. One of the better known historical events relating to skiing took place in 1521 when the future King Gustav Vasa attempted to arouse his countrymen into battle against the controlling Danes. Unfortunately for him, he failed to gather any support and so fled the country on skis. For some reason, after he left his followers changed their minds and decided to fight … except the king was now happily skiing across the mountains. Two men were sent after their leader to convince him to return home and lead the battle, which he did. A year later, Gustav defeated the Danes and was elected king.

King Gustav Vasa's crossing and victory is commemorated each year at the annual Vasaloppet Cross-country Race. The fifty-three-mile event attracts almost 10,000 participants and is the biggest race of its kind.

SKIING ARMY

Skiing was incorporated into some armies as early as the 1200s. Lack of technique and equipment, however, inhibited any real control over early skis, rendering them useless in anything more than a forward shuffle.

The Norwegian army solved some of these problems in 1721 and formed the first organized "ski company." One of the first innovations was the addition of a heel strap to aid in controlling the skis and help make turning possible. A large single pole was also added to the skiers' equipment list and was used by the skier to push himself along flat ground. The pole could also be dragged along when skiing downhill to provide some type of speed control.

The beginning of the nineteenth century saw a plethora of equipment come and go. One style of skiing used one short ski and one long ski. The short ski was used to push and was occasionally wrapped in animal fur to help the ski grip the snow, while the long ski was used to glide. As with many ski styles of the era, a large single pole was carried to aid in control.

JOHN A. "SNOWSHOE" THOMSON

One of the earliest ski "personalities" to emerge in American ski lore was a mail carrier named John A. Thomson. Born in Norway, Thomson immigrated to America in 1837 with his parents.

Thomson began to earn his place in skiing history when he responded to a plea put out by the Sacramento postmaster for someone to carry mail between Placerville, California and Nevada's Carson Valley at the California border. At the time, the ninety-mile trek across the Sierra Nevada was the only means of communication between California and the rest of the Union. Two well-known mountain men of the time had attempted the trip on snowshoes and failed, finding the snow-covered mountains too difficult to traverse even with snowshoes!

Thomson responded to the postmaster's request and made the difficult crossing in three days with the skis he had learned to use as a child in Norway. For the next thirteen years he made the journey countless times, often carrying well over a hundred pounds of correspondence. His worth was considered invaluable during the Civil War years since he supplied the only means of communication between California and the rest of the Union. In addition to carrying the mail, John A. "Snowshoe" Thomson is also credited with numerous mid-winter rescues. Thomson is buried in Genoa, California.

FIRST TECHNIQUES

Three men played an important role in the development of early ski equipment and technique.

Sondre Norheim is considered by many to be the father of the ski technique most used today. Born in Telemark,

Norway around the beginning of the nineteenth century, Sondre Norheim grew up on skis. Seeking to gain greater control over his skis, Sondre fashioned "stiff" bindings out of birch root by soaking the roots and then twisting them into shape and allowing them to dry. His new bindings gave him greater control than had previously been possible, and in 1850 Sondre Norheim became the first skier to make a parallel turn. He also developed the telemark turn, named in honor of his hometown.

Mathias Zdarsky is credited with being the first man to develop an organized ski technique that could be systematically taught to aspiring skiers. Know as the *Lilienfeld Technique*, it involved the use of a single pole, a low body crouch, and one ski in a plow position when going downhill. For the first time in history, novice skiers were able to "ski" downhill with some form of control.

The introduction of "toe irons" by Fritz Huitfeld in the mid-1890s vastly improved the amount of control skiers had over their skis and enhanced Zdarsky's technique even more.

Hannes Schneider, a native of Stuben, Austria, is responsible for introducing recreational downhill skiing to the public. When he began his career as a ski instructor in 1907, Schneider had the foresight to realize that downhill *speed* is what would bring the mass public into the sport of skiing. Basing his technique on the principles introduced by Mathias Zdarsky, Schneider developed a teaching system known as the Arlberg technique. The emphasis was on teaching the novice skier a progressive series of maneuvers based around the stem christie turn.

After World War I, Schneider, working with German filmmaker Dr. Arnold Fanck, made numerous skiing documentaries that were seen worldwide and firmly established the Arlberg technique as *the standard* in ski and teaching technique by the early 1920s.

THE STEEL EDGE

Nineteen hundred and twenty-eight was an important year in the development of ski equipment. It was the year that an enterprising skier named Rudolf Lettner decided to put steel edges on his skis to help protect them from damage. Unfortunately for Rudolf, he didn't feel his "invention" was very impressive or important, so he didn't patent his innovative idea!

It was discovered that adding steel edges greatly added to the amount of control over skis. Prior to the introduction of the steel edge, skiing was limited to soft snow since the skis were incapable of "biting" into hard pack or ice. With steel edges, the skier could ski on a much wider range of conditions, and also was given greatly improved control. Equipment wise, the introduction of the steel edge is one of the innovations that brought skiing into the modern era.

UPHILL TRANSPORTATION

Up until the 1930s, one of the major drawbacks to downhill skiing had always been the fact that one had to walk, ski, or snowshoe up the hill before skiing down the hill was possible. Alex Foster solved the problem when he installed the world's first rope tow at Shawbridge, Quebec, which allowed skiers to be pulled up the hill. Turning skiing into a "downhill only" activity helped attract thousands of people into the sport.

The rope tow made its debut in the United States when the ski area at Woodstock, Vermont installed one in 1934. With the introduction of the rope tow, modern downhill skiing had truly arrived. With downhill-only skiing, the need for a "free" heel for walking was eliminated and new bindings were developed that held the heel in place for greater control.

Soon "Snow Trains" transported city dwellers to ski areas in Vermont and Canada on weekends, and the *weekend ski trip* became a popular American activity.

In 1936, Fred Pabst invented the T-bar, and 1937 saw the installation of the first chairlift at Belknap, New Hampshire.

SUN VALLEY

The 1936 opening of the Sun Valley resort in Idaho brought glamor and luxury to the sport of skiing. Sun Valley featured comfortable chairlifts, first-class accommodations, swimming pools, restaurants, and entertainment. Skiers could now travel to a "ski resort" and enjoy a true vacation without the hardships that previously had been associated with ski areas.

Built by W. Averell Harriman of the Union Pacific Railroad, Sun Valley set the standard for the numerous resorts that were to follow, all of which were inspired by Sun Valley's success. By the end of the 1930s, major ski areas with "modern" lifts were built and developed in California, Utah, New Hampshire, and Vermont, and hundreds of local hills around the country featured rope tows and T-bars. Modern downhill skiing had arrived!

Index

A

Advanced skills, 119-22
Adventure of skiing, 9
Alta, Utah, 143
American Red Cross, 123, 132-3
   CPR classes, 132-3
   first aid class, 123
American Teaching System, 167
Arlberg technique, 176
Aspen, Colorado, 135, 140
Atomic, 17, 18

B

Basic skills, 69-91
Beaver Creek, Colorado, 145
Bindings, 20-1
   din scale, 20
   elasticity, 20
   forward pressure, 20
   full spectrum twincam, 20-1
   maintenance, 21
   operation, 21
   power compensation toe, 21
Birkebeinerrennet Cross-country Race, 174
Blizzard (manufacturer), 17
Boot bag, 16
Boots, 13-5
   cost, 15
   features, 14-5
   mechanical adjustments, 15
Breckenridge, Colorado, 144

C

Children, 147-57
   equipment, 149-50
   fear, 147-8
   games, 156-7
   photo, 148
   ski schools, 150-3
   teaching, 153-4
Clubs, 165-7
   selecting, 166-7
Competition, 11, 169-71

Competition, cont.
   downhill, 171
   giant slalom, 170-1
   Nastar, 169
   slalom, 169-70
Copper Mountain, Colorado, 144

D

Descente (manufacturer), 24
Din scale, 20

E

Edging skis, 106
Emergency phones, photo, 124
Equipment, 13-26, 149-50
   bindings, 20-1
   boot bag, 16
   boots, 13-5
   for children, 149-50
   glasses and goggles, 23-4
   gloves, 22-3
   hats, 23
   long underwear, 25-6
   poles, 22
   ski bag, 21
   ski jackets and parkas, 25
   ski socks, 26
   ski suits, 24-5
   skis, 16-9
Ess/Atomic, 21, see also Atomic
Exercise benefits, 9
Exercises, 27-68
   ankle roll, 38-41
   arm press, 32-3
   arm roll, 30-1
   arm stretch, 37-8
   butt lift, 66
   calf stretch, 44
   head roll, 28-30
   inner thigh stretch, 50-1
   knee bend, 41-2
   knee lift and stretch, 45-6
   leg lifts, 60-4

Exercises, cont.
  leg stretches, 53-60
  push-ups, 67
  relaxing stretch, 68
  shoulder raise, 34
  shoulder roll, 35-6
  sit-ups, 64-5
  skier's hop, 52-3
  skier's knee roll, 42-3
  upper leg stretch, 46-8
  wall sit, 48-50

F
Family participation, 10
Fanck, Arnold, 176
First aid, 123-34
  accident management, 133
  bruises, 131
  cardiopulmonary resuscitation, 132-3
  dislocations and sprains, 130
  eye injuries, 132
  fractures, 128-9
  frostbite, 127-8
  hypothermia, 128
  kit, 133-4
  photo, 131
  severe bleeding, 126-7
  shock, 131-2
  splints, 129-30
  stay with victim, 125
Foster, Alex, 177

G
Getting in shape, 27-68
Geze (manufacturer), 21, 150
Glasses, 23-4
G.L.M., see Graduating Length Method
Gloves, 22-3
Goggles, 23-4
Graduating Length Method, 167
Gustav Vasa, 174

H
Harriman, W. Averell, 177
Hats, 23
Hazards, 98
Heat Factory (manufacturer), 22
Heavenly Valley, California, 141
Helicopter skiing, 98
History of skiing, 173-8
  early skiers, 173-4
  first techniques, 175-6
  skiing army, 174-5
  steel edge, 176-7
  Sun Valley, Idaho, 177-8
  uphill transportation, 177
"Hot Glove," 22-3
Huitfeld, Fritz, 176

I
Instructors, see Schools
Intermediate skills, 105-17

J
Jackson Hole, Wyoming, 139
Jay Peak, Vermont, 145

K
Killington, Vermont, 141
Killy (manufacturer), 24
K2 (manufacturer), 149

L
Lake Louise, Alberta, 143
Lessons, 121-2
Lettner, Rudolf, 176
Lift tickets, 102
Lifts, 94-8
  chairlifts, 96-7
    getting on and off, 97
  gondolas, 98
  helicopters, 98
  J-bar, 95
  poma lift, 95
    photo, 95
  rope tow, 94
  T-bar, 96
Lilienfeld Technique, 176
Look (manufacturer), 21

M
Mammoth, California, 141
Marker (manufacturer), 20, 21, 150
Mental aspects, 159-64
  fear, 163-4
  let it happen, 161
  relaxation, 159-61
  ruts, 162-3
Mont Ste.-Anne, Quebec, 142-3
Mt. Bachelor, Oregon, 143

N
Nastar, 169
Night skiing, 94
Nordica, 15
Norheim, Sondre, 175-6

O
Obermeyer (manufacturer), 24
Okemo, Vermont, 142
Out of bounds, 99

P
Pabst, Fred, 177
Park City, Utah, 141-2
Poles, 22

R

Reasons to ski, 9-11
Relaxation, 10

S

Salomon (manufacturer), 21, 150
Schneider, Hannes, 176
Schools, 165-7
    private or group lessons, 165-6
    selecting, 166-7
Schweitzer Mountain Resort, Idaho, 139
Signs, 99-101
Ski bag, 21
Ski jackets and parkas, 25
Ski Magazine, 150, 169
Ski patrol, 99, 125
    photo, 125
Ski schools for children, 150-3
    photo, 151
Ski suits, 24-5
    jump suits, 24
    snow pants, 24-5
Skiing, as money-making activity, 11
Skiing environment, 93-104
Skill level signs, 99-100
Skills, advanced, 119-22
    jumping, 121
    moguls, 120
    powder, 119-20
    skiing on ice, 119
    speed, 120-1
Skills, basic, 69-91
    basic skiing position, 70
    falling, 85-7
    getting up, 87-9
    gliding, 73-4
    herringbone walk, 75-6
    kick turn, 81-4
    side slipping, 79-81
    sidestepping, 76-8
    skating with skis, 72-3
    snowplow, 89-91
    walking with skis, 70-1
Skills, intermediate, 105-17
    check, 115
    connecting parallel turns, 115
    edging skis, 106
    finishing turns, 105
    parallel stop, 115-7
    parallel turn, 112-4
    snowplow turn, 106-8
    stem christie turn, 110-12
    traversing, 109-10
    unweighting, 105-6
Skis, 16-9, 70-1, 72-3
    features, 18-9

Skis, features, cont.
    camber, 18-9
    damping ability, 19
    flex, 19
    length, 18
    side camber or sidecut, 19
    torsional stiffness, 19
    skating with, 72-3
    types, 16-8
        all terrain, 18
        downhill, 18
        giant slalom, 17
        light expert, 18
        mogul, 17
        novice or learner, 16-7
        powder, 18
        recreational, 17
        slalom, 17
        sport, 17
    walking with, 70-1
Sno-Zone, 23
Snow, types of, 102-4
Snowcats, 93-4
Snowmass, Colorado, 140
Snowplow, 89-91
Snowplow turn, 106-8
Social activity, 10
Socks, 26
Squaw Valley, California, 144
Stem christie turn, 110-12
Sun Valley, Idaho, 139-40, 177-8

T

Teaching, 154-6
Thomson, John A. "Snowshoe," 175
Trail maps, 101-2
Travel, 10, 136
    photo, 136
Traversing, 109-10
Tyrolia (manufacturer), 21, 149, 150

U

Underwear, long, 25-6
Unweighting, 105-6
Uvex (manufacturer), 24

V

Vacations, 135-45
Vail, Colorado, 142
Vasaloppet Cross-country Race, 174

W

Whistler/Blackcomb, British Columbia, 144
Winter Park, Colorado, 142

Z

Zdarsky, Mathias, 176